Duden

150 Englischübungen

5. bis 10. Klasse

Regeln und Texte zum Üben

Mit Illustrationen von Steffen Butz

Dudenverlag
Mannheim • Leipzig • Wien • Zürich

Bibliografische Informationen der Deutschen Nationalbibliothek
Die Deutsche Nationalbibliothek verzeichnet diese Publikation in der Deutschen Nationalbibliografie; detaillierte bibliografische Daten sind im Internet über http://dnb.ddb.de abrufbar.

Redaktionelle Leitung Annika Renker
Redaktion Linda Strehl
Sprecher Alison Rippier, Michael Shiels

Herstellung Annette Scheerer
Layout Horst Bachmann
Illustration Steffen Butz
Umschlaggestaltung Michael Acker
Umschlagfoto Fotostudio Kauffelt, Mannheim
Umschlagillustration Steffen Butz

Satz Elstersatz, Stefan Hergenröder, Wildflecken
Druck und Bindung Firmengruppe APPL, Wemding
Printed in Germany

ISBN 978-3-411-73321-7

Inhalt

Empfohlen für: 5 = 5. Klasse 6 = 6. Klasse 7–8 = 7. bis 8. Klasse usw.

9 Wortschatz

10 Umgang mit Texten

Lösungen

Empfohlen für: 5 = 5. Klasse 6 = 6. Klasse 7–8 = 7. bis 8. Klasse usw.

INHALT

Liebe Schülerin, lieber Schüler!

Die englische Grammatik und die zugehörigen unzähligen Regeln und Begriffe bereiten dir immer wieder Schwierigkeiten? Mach dir nichts daraus, denn Englisch kann man üben. Mit diesem Buch bist du auf dem richtigen Weg dazu. Der Schwerpunkt dieses Bandes ist das Üben – mehr als 150 abwechslungsreiche Aufgaben ermöglichen dir, dich auf die Klassenarbeit vorzubereiten und Englisch zu trainieren. Dabei kannst du diejenigen Problemfelder, die dir besondere Schwierigkeiten bereiten, ganz gezielt angehen. Die Kapitel greifen alle Gebiete der englischen Grammatik auf, die du von der 5. bis zur 10. Klasse beherrschen musst.

Infokästen

In den Kästen, die den einzelnen Kapiteln und Unterkapiteln vorangestellt sind, findest du kurze Regeln und Merksätze. Sie liefern den Stoff, den du aus der Schule kennst, in kleinen Portionen zum Auffrischen und Wiederholen. Oft gibt es hier auch wertvolle Tipps und natürlich Beispiele. Danach kannst du das Wissen aus den Infokästen mit den nachfolgenden Aufgaben üben.
Merke dir: Es ist nicht wichtig, dass du die Regeln auswendig lernst, sondern dass du sie anwendest und durch **Übung** zum Meister wirst!

Es gibt ganz unterschiedliche Arten von Übungen. Manche trainieren nur die Formen, andere helfen dir, deinen Stil im Englischen zu verbessern. Dadurch probst du den Ernstfall und die unterschiedlichen Übungsformen in der Schule. Viele der Aufgaben kannst du direkt im Buch bearbeiten, für die anderen legst du dir am besten ein eigenes Übungsheft an.
Wichtig ist im Englischen natürlich auch, dass du dein Hörverständnis trainierst. Deshalb findest du im Buch immer wieder Übungen mit dem CD-Symbol. Hier kannst du mit der beigefügten CD Übungen zum „listening comprehension" machen.
Damit du dich gut zurechtfinden kannst, steht in der Randspalte die **Klassenstufe,** für die die Aufgaben am besten geeignet sind. Dies ist aber nur eine grobe Einordnung zur ersten Orientierung, schließlich unterrichtet nicht

jeder Lehrer gleich, und oft werden in späteren Jahrgängen Dinge noch einmal wiederholt und erneut abgefragt. Deshalb spricht überhaupt nichts dagegen, dass du auch Aufgaben der anderen Klassen übst. Je mehr Übungen du bearbeitest, desto schneller wirst du besser. Am hilfreichsten ist es sicherlich, wenn du dich zuerst an den Übungen zu denjenigen Themenfeldern versuchst, die ihr gerade im Unterricht behandelt. Falls du dir nicht sicher bist, kannst du deinen Lehrer / deine Lehrerin fragen.
Die ausführlichen **Lösungen** zu den Übungen sowie die Texte zum Hörverständnis von der CD findest du nach dem 10. Kapitel am Ende des Buches. Auf der letzten Seite kannst du mithilfe des **Registers** auch nach einzelnen Stichwörtern suchen.

Der Ernstfall – Englisch als Klassenarbeit oder Test

Es gibt ein paar allgemeine Regeln, die du beachten kannst:

1. Bevor es losgeht, solltest du überprüfen, ob genügend Tinte im Füller ist. Schau außerdem, ob noch ausreichend Platz in deinem Heft ist. Lege eventuell ein Zusatzheft oder leere Blätter bereit. Konzentriere dich dann ganz auf die Arbeit. Sei ruhig und gelassen, schließlich hast du geübt!
2. Lies die Aufgabenstellungen in Ruhe durch und mach dir klar, was von dir verlangt wird. Erste „Geistesblitze" kannst du dir schon jetzt notieren.
3. Mach dich nun an das Beantworten der Fragen. Lies dir das Ergebnis anschließend in Ruhe durch und mach noch letzte Verbesserungen.
4. Überprüfe auch, ob sich Rechtschreib- und Flüchtigkeitsfehler eingeschlichen haben. Korrigiere diese und gib dann ab.

Alle weiteren wichtigen Punkte, die speziell für die verschiedenen Gebiete der Grammatik gelten, findest du nun in den folgenden Kapiteln ausführlich behandelt.

Viel Spaß beim Trainieren!
Und beim Besserwerden!

1

Substantive und Artikel

1.1 Der Plural

Regelmäßige und unregelmäßige Pluralformen

Die regelmäßigen Pluralformen *(regular plural forms)* werden gebildet, indem du ein ***-s*** an das Substantiv anhängst: *team* ⟶ *teams.*
Endet ein Substantiv auf einem Zischlaut ([dʒ], [tʃ], [ks]), hängst du ***-es*** an: *watch* ⟶ *watches* (Aussprache [ɪz]). Endet ein Substantiv auf einen Konsonanten + *y*, lautet die Pluralendung ***-ies:*** *baby* ⟶ *babies.*
Bei manchen Substantiven auf *-f* oder *-fe* wird der Plural mit *-ves* gebildet: *shelf* ⟶ *shelves;* bestimmte Substantive auf *-o* hängen im Plural *-es* an: *tomato* ⟶ *tomatoes.*
Einige wenige Substantive haben unregelmäßige Pluralformen *(irregular plural forms)*, die du auswendig lernen musst.

1 **Setze die Substantive in Klammern in der richtigen Form ein.**

My favourite hobby is hockey. Two ______________ (coach) train our team on Wednesday afternoons. On Saturdays we usually play two ______________ (match).
In each team there are eleven ______________ (player) and we all have hockey ______________ (stick). Our players wear green ______________ (T-shirt) and we all have special ______________ (shoe).
A lot of ______________ (friend) and ______________ (family) come to watch the matches. After the matches we often have dinner together. I usually eat two or three ______________ (sandwich) and drink two small ______________ (bottle) of coke. I'm always

very hungry after the matches. Sometimes my mother brings two

big ______________ (cake). They are yummy!

What are your ______________ (hobby)?

2 **Bilde den Plural der folgenden Wörter und sortiere sie je nach der Aussprache in die passende Spalte.**

house – friend – book – window – bed – chocolate – orange – banana – shop – snake – cage – watch

a) [z]	**b)** [ɪz]	**c)** [s]
______________	______________	______________
______________	______________	______________
______________	______________	______________
______________	______________	______________

3 **Wie lautet die Pluralform der folgenden Substantive?**

man	______________	child	______________
sandwich	______________	knife	______________
baby	______________	box	______________
boy	______________	potato	______________
woman	______________	house	______________
class	______________	tooth	______________

1.2 Paarwörter und nicht zählbare Substantive

Plural- oder Singularform?

Einige Substantive werden nur im Plural verwendet. Dazu gehören die **Paarwörter** *(pair nouns)*. Diese Substantive bezeichnen Dinge, die aus zwei gleichen Teilen bestehen: *trousers*. Bei Paarwörtern steht auch das Verb im Plural. Paarwörter können nicht mit *a/an* oder *one/two/three* verbunden werden. Willst du ein Paarwort zählbar machen, musst du es mit *a/one pair of, two pairs of, three pairs of* ... verbinden.
Einige Wörter existieren nur im Singular. Es sind **nicht zählbare Substantive** *(uncountable nouns)*, die man nicht zählen und nicht in die Pluralform setzen kann: *food, music*. Diese Wörter musst du auswendig lernen. Die unzählbaren Substantive können nicht mit *a/an* oder *one/two/three* verbunden werden. Willst du sie zählbar machen, brauchst du eine entsprechende Ergänzung: *a cup of tea*.

4 **Übersetze die folgenden Sätze ins Englische.**

a) Deine neue Brille ist hübsch.

____

b) Meine Hausaufgaben waren leicht.

____

c) Wo ist meine Jeans?

____

d) Ich habe keine Schere.

____

e) Peter hat zwei blaue Hosen.

____

5 **Lies die Sätze und unterstreiche die richtige Form.**

a) Do you really want to wear a jeans/some jeans?

b) Where did you get this/these fantastic headphones?

c) Many/Much thanks for your help.

d) You can always buy another shorts/another pair of shorts.

e) Where is/are my pyjamas? – I think I've already packed them/it.

f) £ 15 for a pair of scissors/a scissors! It is/They are really expensive.

6 **Finde die Fehler in den folgenden Sätzen und schreibe den verbesserten Satz in dein Übungsheft. Achtung: Einige Sätze sind korrekt!**

a) Do you want coffee?
b) I haven't got a pen.
c) Sarah drinks a water every day.
d) My friends often listen to music when they work.
e) Look at all those hairs on your new anorak.
f) We need a milk and four eggs.
g) Would you like some breads?

7 **Übersetze die folgenden Sätze ins Englische und schreibe sie in dein Übungsheft.**

a) Ich brauche eine neue Strumpfhose und einen Schlafanzug.
b) Es sind heute viele Leute im Park.
c) Trägt Liz gewöhnlich eine Brille?
d) Meine Familie trinkt jeden Tag mehrere Flaschen Wasser.
e) Ich hätte gerne Schokolade und etwas Brot.

1.3 Der Genitiv

Der *s*-Genitiv und die *of*-Fügung

Um auszudrücken, dass etwas oder jemand zu einer Person gehört, verwendet man den ***s*-Genitiv:** *Jill's car.*
Wenn etwas mehreren Personen gehört, hängt man einen Apostroph an die Pluralform an: *the boys' books.* Bei den unregelmäßigen Pluralformen hängt man einen Apostroph + *s* an: *the children's toys.*
Um auszudrücken, dass etwas oder jemand zu einer Sache gehört, verwendet man die ***of*-Fügung:** *the colour of his T-shirt.*

8 **Übersetze die farbig markierten Satzteile.**

a) Du kannst dir Lucys Bücher ausleihen.

___

b) Das Auto der Johnsons ist nagelneu.

___

c) Der Lehrer der Schüler kommt aus Kanada.

___

d) Glaubst du, Mr. Smiths Sohn kommt in unsere Klasse?

___

e) Die Farbe deiner Augen ist schwer zu bestimmen.

___

f) Der Fernseher der Familie ist schon seit Wochen kaputt.

___

g) Das Ende des Spiels steht unmittelbar bevor.

___

9 **Bilde den Genitiv Plural.**

Singular	Plural
the boy's class	______________
the school's buildings	______________
the man's job	______________
the girl's room	______________
the child's toys	______________
the woman's hair	______________
the family's cars	______________

10 **Das Computerprogramm hat in Bens Aufsatz Apostrophe und das Genitiv-*s* verschluckt. Füge sie an der richtigen Stelle ein.**

We moved into our new house. It is fantastic. Now I have my own little room. My two brother_____ Tim and Joe also have their own rooms. But my two sister_____ share a big room. My sister_____ room is next to mine and my parent_____ bedroom is also on the first floor. My brother_____ rooms are downstairs. Blacky_____ basket is in the hall right next to Tim and Joe_____ room, so he doesn't have to sleep in the garage. My dad_____ office and my mum_____ reading room are also on the ground floor. And the garage is big enough for my parent_____ car, my brother_____ bikes and the children_____ toys.

1.4 Der Artikel

Der bestimmte und der unbestimmte Artikel

Im Englischen steht der **bestimmte Artikel** *(definite article) the,* wenn eine Person/Sache näher bestimmt ist, abstrakte Begriffe durch einen Relativsatz oder eine *of-phrase* näher bestimmt sind, und bei Institutionen, wenn das Gebäude gemeint ist. Er steht nicht bei abstrakten Begriffen im allgemeinen Sinn, bei Institutionen, wenn die Funktion gemeint ist, bei Monaten, Wochentagen, Feiertagen und Mahlzeiten.
Den **unbestimmten Artikel** *(indefinite article) a* (vor Konsonant) und *an* (vor Vokal) benutzt du, wenn keine bestimmte Person oder Sache gemeint ist, bei Nationalitäten, Berufen und Verbindungen mit *half, quite, such* und *what*.

11 **Vervollständige die Sätze mit dem bestimmten Artikel dort, wo er nötig ist.**

a) ________ Life/life in England wasn't easy in the 16th century, not even ________ life of a king or queen.

b) ________ School/school that I go to has a lot of pupils. I don't like big schools. Well, I don't like ________ school anyway, but my parents think that ________ school is important for my future.

c) ________ People/people who live in our street are usually very loud. ________ People/people can be so unfriendly.

d) Sarah lives in a big town. There's a prison and a university. She goes to ________ university because she wants to become a doctor. ________ Prison/prison is not far from ________ university.

12 ***The, a/an*** **oder kein Artikel – entscheide dich.**

a) Bill takes ______ bath every morning and has cornflakes for ______ breakfast.

b) Jenny can't go to ______ school today. She has got ______ headache and ______ temperature.

c) Poor/______ poor Tim. He broke his leg after ______ breakfast.

d) Jane likes music. In ______ afternoons she often plays ______ guitar.

e) We usually go on holiday in ______ July.

f) What ______ lovely day! The sun is shining, so we can go outside.

g) Janet wants to become ______ teacher.

13 **Vervollständige die folgenden Sätze, indem du die passenden Begriffe in den Wortspeichern zusammenfügst. Schreibe sie in dein Übungsheft.**

quite – such – half – what – such – quite	a beautiful dress – a stupid thing to do – an easy question – a lovely meal – a useful thing – an hour later

I have never eaten ...
Look at these clothes. ...
Tim, you must be more careful. It was ...
It was raining heavily, but ... it stopped suddenly.
We can do our homework quickly. It is ...
A penknife is ... because you can take it everywhere.

2

Pronomen

2.1 Personalpronomen

Ersetzung von Substantiven in Subjekt- und Objektform

Substantive können durch Personalpronomen *(personal pronouns)* ersetzt werden. Bei Gegenständen steht immer das Personalpronomen *it*.

1 **Höre dir Track 1 auf der CD an und füge die Subjektform des Personalpronomens in die Lücken ein.** 1

Hi, my name is Sue. _______ am eleven years old. My dad is called Adam. _______ is 40 years old. My mother's name is Carole. _______ is 36 years old. _______ are both teachers. _______ have two brothers. _______ are six and eight years old. We live in a very busy street but _______ have a nice garden. _______ is quite big. _______ can play football there. _______ can visit me here! _______ are always welcome.

2 **Ersetze die farbigen Satzteile durch Personalpronomen in der Objektform.**

a) The teacher tells the children to be quiet. _______________

b) The teacher is giving Sarah a book. _______________

c) Can you help Peter? _______________

d) Please give the book to your sister. _______________

e) The neighbours are helping our family. _______________

f) Can you ask Peter and Sarah? _______________

2.2 Possessivbegleiter und -pronomen

Besitzanzeigende Fürwörter

Possessivbegleiter *(possessive determiners)* zeigen an, **wem oder zu wem etwas gehört.** Sie stehen direkt vor Substantiven.
Possessivpronomen *(possessive pronouns)* zeigen ebenfalls an, wem etwas gehört, im Unterschied zu den Possessivbegleitern stehen sie jedoch allein und ersetzen das Substantiv.

3 **Ersetze die farbigen Satzteile mit dem richtigen Possessivbegleiter.**

a) Peter's bike	___________ bike
b) my mother's shoes	___________ shoes
c) Kate and Sue's basketball	___________ basketball
d) the horse's saddle	___________ saddle
e) Carole's diary *(Tagebuch)*	___________ diary

4 **Wähle den passenden Possessivbegleiter aus und füge ihn ein.**

Carole is looking for ___________ (his/her/its) shoes. ___________ (his/her/their) brother is helping her. They are looking in ___________ (our/their/her) bedrooms and in ___________ (her/your/their) parents' bedroom, but they can't find them anywhere. Carole tells ___________ (her/his/our) mother: "We're looking for ___________ (their/my/our) shoes!" – "Ask ___________ (her/his/your) grandpa. He's in ___________ (her/their/his) room. Maybe he knows where your shoes are."

5 **Thomas erzählt seinem Vater von der neuen Schule. Fülle die Lücken mit den fehlenden Pronomen.**

Mr Simpson: "Hi Tom. How was the first day at __________ (deiner) new school?"

Tom: "Hi dad. __________ new school is not too bad. My classmates are friendly and __________ (unser) classroom is nice, too. __________ (Es) is a big room with lots of posters. __________ (Seine) windows are also big, so we can look outside when the lessons are boring."

Mr Simpson: "Oh dear. Are __________ (deine) new teachers so boring?"

Tom: "Well, __________ (unsere) English teacher, Miss Evans, is nice. __________ (ihre) two sons are in __________ (meiner) class as well. __________ (Ihr) table is next to __________ (meinem)."

6 **Übersetze die markierten Satzteile ins Englische. Schreibe in dein Übungsheft.**

a) Ich bat sie (meine Geschwister) um Hilfe.
b) Bitte lass den Kuchen stehen. Das ist unserer.
c) John brach sich beim Fußballspielen das Bein.
d) Wo ist euer Lehrer?
e) Hier ist ein Geldbeutel. Ist das deiner?
f) Die Maus frisst ihren Käse.
g) Ms Williams hat ihre Tasche verloren.

2.3 Demonstrativpronomen

Hinweisende Fürwörter

Mit Demonstrativpronomen *(demonstrative pronouns)* weist man auf etwas hin. ***This*** und ***these*** werden für Personen oder Dinge verwendet, die sich in der näheren Umgebung des Sprechers befinden, ***that*** und ***those*** für Personen oder Dinge, die sich in weiterer Entfernung befinden. Bei diesen Demonstrativpronomen steht oft *over there*.

7 **Hannah kauft ein. Ergänze die Demonstrativpronomen und achte darauf, ob die Dinge näher oder weiter entfernt vom Sprecher sind. Dies erkennst du an den Signalwörtern.**

Hannah: "Could I have one kilo of potatoes, please?"

Mrs Rose: "Sure. Would you like __________ new potatoes here or __________ sweet potatoes over there?"

Hannah: "__________ new potatoes, please. Are __________ apples sweet?"

Mrs Rose: "Oh, they're okay. But __________ apples over there are lovely."

Hannah: "OK, I'll have six apples then and __________ watermelon over there. What is __________ round fruit here?"

Mrs Rose: "Oh, __________ is a mango. Try it! Mangos taste delicious."

Hannah: "Okay, one mango, please. And I'll also have a few of __________ bananas over there."

5. KLASSE

2.4 Reflexivpronomen

Rückbezügliche Pronomen

Die Reflexivpronomen *(reflexive pronouns)*, gebildet mit ***-self/-selves,*** beziehen sich auf das Subjekt eines Satzes zurück: Das Objekt bezeichnet also dieselbe Person wie das Subjekt. Sie werden auch verwendet, wenn man ein Substantiv oder Pronomen eines Satzes hervorheben will. Viele Verben, die im Deutschen reflexiv sind, werden im Englischen nicht reflexiv gebraucht.

8 **Setze die richtigen Reflexivpronomen ein.**

a) He was looking at ________________ in the mirror.

b) I'm not angry with you. I'm angry with ________________.

c) My parents enjoyed ________________ in New York.

d) We are old enough to look after ________________.

e) The food is on the table. Just help ________________, boys!

f) I didn't buy those pies. I made them ________________.

9 **In jedem der folgenden Sätze ist ein Fehler. Markiere ihn und verbessere ihn in deinem Übungsheft. Aufgepasst: Ein Satz ist richtig!**

a) We are late, so we must hurry ourselves.
b) Be careful, don't cut you with that bread knife.
c) Her friend is really nice now. He has changed himself a lot.
d) My mum always worries when I'm with my friends.
e) Can I get me a drink?
f) I can't remember myself. I've never seen that film before.

10 **Lies die Sätze durch, suche ein passendes Verb aus und entscheide, wo das Verb ein Reflexivpronomen benötigt.**

to help – to enjoy – to hide – to meet – to open – to relax – to move – to do

a) The door ______________________, and a girl walks in.

b) You must be tired. Just ______________________

and ______________________.

c) They ________________ the exercises ____________________.

d) Are we ______________________ at 7 o'clock for dinner?

e) Look at that car over there. It is ______________________.

f) We ______________________ to some drinks and sandwiches.

g) Where ___________ you __________________? I can't see you!

11 **Übersetze die Sätze in deinem Übungsheft ins Englische und benutze das richtige Reflexivpronomen. Achtung: Nicht immer muss im Englischen das Reflexivpronomen stehen!**

a) Ich habe dieses Buch selbst gekauft.
b) Sei vorsichtig mit dem neuen Messer. Du kannst dich schneiden.
c) Wir müssen uns keine Sorgen machen.
d) Wir haben uns sehr amüsiert.
e) Setzen Sie sich bitte und machen Sie sich keine Sorgen.
f) Er beeilte sich, weil er sich im Dunkeln fürchtete.

2.5 Reziproke Pronomen und das Stützwort *one/ones*

Gegenseitige Handlungen

Each other und ***one another*** sind reziproke Pronomen *(reciprocal pronouns)*. Sie werden verwendet, wenn eine Handlung auf Gegenseitigkeit beruht: *We send each other birthday cards every year.*
Soll ein zählbares Substantiv nicht wiederholt werden, so kann es durch das Stützwort *(prop-word)* ***one/ones*** ersetzt werden. Der bestimmte Artikel oder Adjektive können – anders als im Deutschen – nicht allein stehen. Sie benötigen *one/ones* als Stützwort: *I have a red bike and a green one.*

12 **Vervollständige die Sätze unten mit den Satzteilen im Wortspeicher. Achtung: reziprokes Pronomen oder Reflexivpronomen?**

look after each other – look after themselves – talk to each other – talk to themselves – help each other – help yourselves

a) When old friends meet, they often ____________________

____________________.

b) Young and fit people can ______________________________.

c) People who live alone often start to ____________________

____________________.

d) First she was ill in bed, then he was ill, so they had to

____.

e) Fred and Sheila phone every day to ____________________

____________________.with their homework.

f) Please ______________________________. Everything you need

is on the table.

13 **Vervollständige die Sätze, indem du das Stützwort *one/ones* benutzt.**

a) Can you lend me your pen? – Sorry, I haven't got __________.

b) This cup is dirty. Can I have a clean ____________?

c) Which trousers do you like? These ____________ or those ____________?

d) This box is too small. I need a bigger ____________.

e) Those shoes are much nicer than the blue ____________.

14 **Entscheide dich für das richtige Pronomen und unterstreiche es.**

a) Friends usually give themselves/each other presents at Christmas.

b) Anna and I don't see us/ourselves/each other very often.

c) My brother always cuts his hair –/himself.

d) Stop talking about you/–/yourself. That's boring.

e) He can't imagine –/himself what might happen next.

15 **Bilde Sätze. Ergänze das fehlende Reflexivpronomen, reziproke Pronomen oder Stützwort, falls notwendig. Achte auch auf die richtige Satzstellung. Schreibe in dein Übungsheft.**

a) Cats/to clean/every day
b) Mike/to enjoy/usually/at parties
c) I/not to feel/very well/at the moment
d) Pat and Jill/to understand/without saying anything
e) There/to be/red apple and/a green
f) Sally's friends/to play with/often/a game of cards

3

Adjektive und Adverbien

3.1 Vergleiche mit Adjektiven

Gleichheit und Ungleichheit

Eine **Gleichheit** wird mit *as* + Adjektiv + *as* („genauso ... wie") ausgedrückt. Eine **Ungleichheit** wird entweder mit der Konstruktion Komparativ + *than* („als") oder *not as/so ... as* („nicht so ... wie") wiedergegeben. Mit *the* + Komparativ ... *the* + Komparativ übersetzt du „je ... desto/umso".

1 **Vervollständige die Sätze mit *as* oder *than*.**

a) I don't watch TV as much ___________ you.

b) You can eat more sandwiches ___________ me.

c) Jim isn't as clever ___________ he thinks.

d) Switzerland is smaller ___________ Germany.

e) The boys couldn't wait longer ___________ an hour.

f) Is your brother older ___________ my brother?

g) Mexico isn't as big ___________ Canada.

2 **Übersetze die deutschen Ausdrücke in den Klammern ins Englische. Schreibe in dein Übungsheft.**

(Je länger) you sleep, (umso müder) you get.
(Je müder) you are, (desto schwieriger) it is to get up.

2

3 **Höre dir Track 2 auf der CD an und vervollständige die Postkarte, die Tina ihrer Freundin Pat aus Schottland geschrieben hat.**

Dear Pat,

Scotland is great, it is ______________________ Wales,

something I think it is even ______________________ Wales.

But I don't know. I guess, I like both parts of the U.K. the same. Yesterday

I went climbing. It was ______________________

I thought. We had to climb up very high but ______________________

Snowdon. I was pretty exhausted, almost ______________________

the time we went rowing on the lake. Do you remember? I'm going

pony trekking with some of the girls at the weekend. I think pony

trekking is ______________________

mountain biking.

______________________ I stay, ______________________

______________ it is getting here in Scotland. And the people here are

even ______________________ back home in Wales. But the summers

here seem to be ______________________

they are in Wales. I hope your holidays

aren't ______________________ they

were last year.

Love,

Tina

3.2 Adjektive als Substantive

Substantivierung durch *the*

Adjektive können im Englischen als Substantiv verwendet werden, wenn *the* vorangestellt wird. Sie bezeichnen dann eine Gruppe oder eine Gesamtheit von Personen: *the blind* („die Blinden“). Dieses Adjektiv hat dann kein Plural-*s*, das Verb steht jedoch im Plural.
Sind einzelne Personen gemeint, muss das Adjektiv **durch ein Substantiv** wie *person, man, girl* usw. **ergänzt** werden: *the blind boy*.

4 **Übersetze und schreibe in dein Übungsheft.**

der Kleine	ein Kranker	die Obdachlosen
die Tote	zwei Schwarze	die Schwachen
der Starke	die Weißen	die Große

5 **Ergänze die Sätze mit der Übersetzung der angegebenen Ausdrücke.**

ein alter Mann – eine reiche Frau – die Armen – ein Blinder – junge Leute

a) There are some good programmes for ______________ on TV.

b) There lives ______________________ over there in that huge bungalow.

c) ______________ was standing at the side of the road with his guide dog.

d) The car has just hit ____________________ who was crossing the street rather slowly.

e) Many people have no idea of the problems ________________ in big cities have.

3.3 Adverbien

Arten der Adverbbildung

Adverbien *(adverbs)* **beschreiben** eine **Tätigkeit** näher: Mit ihnen gibt man an, wie oder auf welche Weise man etwas macht.
Sie werden gebildet, indem man ***-ly*** an das Adjektiv anhängt. Einige Sonderformen musst du beachten: Endet das Adjektiv auf *-y*, lautet die Adverbendung *-ily*, endet es auf *-le*, lautet sie *-ly*, und bei *-ic* steht in der Adverbform *-ically; good* verändert sich zu *well*. Daneben gibt es einige Adjektive, die als Adverb ihre Form nicht verändern. Lerne sie auswendig.

6 **Ergänze die Tabelle mit den richtigen Adverbformen.**

to watch	carefully	more carefully	most carefully
to cycle	well		
to speak		more clearly	
to write		worse	
to speak	slowly		
to play			best
to talk		more loudly	

7 **Wandle die Aussagen in Sätze mit Adverbien um. Schreibe in dein Übungsheft.**
Beispiel: ***James is a careful driver. → James drives carefully.***

a) Betty is a perfect tennis player.
b) John is a nervous speaker.
c) They are careful readers.
d) Christy is a good dancer.
e) The rain is heavy in October.
f) You're a fantastic cook.

8 **Setze die passende Form ein. Achte auf eventuelle Steigerungsformen!**

a) Jenny feels ________________ (besser als) yesterday but not ____________ (gut) enough to go to school.

b) Sarah looked around ________________ (nervös) and started to speak ________________ (leise).

c) Bob opened Nasreen's letter ________________. It was a ____________ (lang) letter in _____________________ (wunderschön) handwriting.

d) Mum drives ___________________ (schneller als) dad. She is not ___________________ (so vorsichtig wie) dad.

e) The police did a ____________ (gut) job. They did their job very ____________ (gut).

f) Carolyn is an opera singer. She sings ____________________ (schön). _____________________________ (so schön wie) a canary *(Kanarienvogel)*.

9 **Übersetze die Sätze. Achte auf die Satzstellung und alle Besonderheiten! Schreibe sie in dein Übungsheft.**

a) Richard öffnet seine Tasche langsam.
b) Mein Vater ist ein vorsichtiger Fahrer.
c) Es ist ein schneller Zug. Er fährt *(to travel)* sehr schnell.
d) Betty ist ziemlich klug.
e) Harry arbeitet sehr hart. Er schläft kaum.
f) Jim tanzt sehr gut. Er ist ein guter Tänzer.

Verben und Zeitformen

4.1 Das *present tense*

Simple present und _present progressive_

Das ***simple present*** entspricht der Grundform des Verbs. In der 3. Person Singular wird immer ein *-s* angehängt: *I send, he sends.* Manche Wörter ändern dabei ihre Schreibweise: *she goes.*
Es steht, wenn etwas regelmäßig, häufig, nie oder immer geschieht. Signalwörter: *always, never, often, sometimes, usually, on (Mondays), every (weekend).*
Das ***present progressive*** bildet man, indem man eine Personalform von *to be* verwendet und an die Grundform des Verbs *-ing* hängt: *I am working, we are reading.*
Es bezeichnet eine Handlung, die im Augenblick des Sprechens gerade abläuft oder noch nicht abgeschlossen ist. Signalwörter: *at the moment, just, now, still, right now.*
Verben der Sinneswahrnehmung stehen normalerweise nicht in der Verlaufsform.

1 ***Simple present* oder *present progressive?***

It's Monday morning. Sandra usually ____________ (go) to school on weekdays. But today she ____________ (stay) at home because she ____________ (have) a bad headache.
Mrs Summer usually ____________ (work) three days a week in a bookstore. This week, however, she ____________ (work) five days because her boss is on holidays. She ____________ just ____________ (sell) a book to a woman.
Sandra's brother Peter sometimes ____________ (write) a letter to his Grandma. Right now, he ____________ (talk) to her on the phone.

It's Friday. Sandra ________ (be) at school. She ____________ (write) a maths test just at the moment. Sandra ____________ (feel) tired, but she ______________ (not/must/go) home yet *(darf noch nicht)*.

Mrs Summer usually ____________ (read) a book on Saturdays. But today she ______________ (watch) TV because it's the Queen's birthday.

On Sundays Sandra's brother Peter usually ____________ (play) football with his friends. But today they ____________ (play) hockey instead.

2 **Setze die verneinten Formen von *simple present* und *present progressive* ein.**

	simple present	**present progressive**
he works	he doesn't work	he isn't working
we talk	______________________	______________________
you run	______________________	______________________
she eats	______________________	______________________
I come	______________________	______________________
we start	______________________	______________________
they play	______________________	______________________
he drives	______________________	______________________
it swims	______________________	______________________

3 **Bilde verneinte Sätze. Beispiel: Lily sleeps in her bed. ⟶ Lily doesn't sleep in the classroom.**

Lily does her homework in her room. But she ____________________ (not/do) her homework in the classroom.

Lily can watch TV in her room. But she _________________________ (not/can/watch) TV in the classroom.

She reads a book in her room every evening. But she __________________ ________ (not/read) her book in the classroom.

At home, Lily can listen to music. But at school, she _____________ _____________ (not/can/listen) to music.

Lily has got a rug *(Teppich)* in her room. But she _____________ ____________ (not/have) a rug in the classroom.

Lily likes her room at home. But she __________________________ (not/like) the classroom.

4 ***Simple*** **oder** ***progressive*** **– Unterstreiche die richtige Form des** ***present tense*****.**

a) What time do you usually get up/are you usually getting up?

b) Kim isn't at home. She is going shopping/goes shopping.

c) Oh look! It snows/is snowing again.

d) Jeff is still working/still works on his project in geography.

e) My parents never eat/are never eating in a restaurant.

f) Mary doesn't take/isn't taking the dog for a walk on Saturdays.

5 ***Simple present* oder *progressive?* Wähle die richtige Form des Verbs.**

a) Whenever Judy's father ________________ (come) home from work, his daughter ________________ (watch) TV. She ________________ (love) soap operas.

b) Hey, just have a look! Sam ________________ (dance) again.

c) I ________________ (wish) I could stay up here forever.

d) Come on! Let's go home. It ________________ (get) dark.

e) They ________________ (do) a lot of hiking these holidays.

f) I ________ (like) that dress you ________________ (wear) today.

g) To the postman's horror, a big, angry-looking dog ________________ (bark) at him.

h) Don't worry! Our dog ________________ (not/bite).

i) Quiet, John, please! Our neighbour ________________ (play) the piano. He ________________ (usually/play) it most beautifully. It simply ________________ (sound) lovely.

j) Jane is terribly cold. She ________________ (shake) all over.

6 **Übersetze und schreibe die Sätze in dein Übungsheft.**

a) Es regnet oft in Irland.
b) Francis geht nicht gerne einkaufen.
c) Bob ruft mich aber auch immer am Abend an.
d) Spielt unser Team diesen Sommer wirklich gut?
e) Die Sonne scheint und es wird heiß.
f) Robert steht auf, geht ins Badezimmer und duscht.

4.2 Das *past tense*

Simple past und past progressive

Beim ***simple past*** der regelmäßigen Verben hängst du *-ed* an die Grundform: *listen → listened.* Viele Verben werden unregelmäßig gebildet und müssen auswendig gelernt werden: *sing → sang; forget → forgot.*
Das *simple past* beschreibt eine in der Vergangenheit abgeschlossene Handlung. Signalwörter: *yesterday, ago,* Zeitangaben mit *last, in* + Jahreszahl.
Das ***past progressive*** bildest du mit *was/were* und der Grundform des Verbs + *-ing: I was doing, you were sleeping.* Es wird verwendet, um ein Ereignis zu beschreiben, das in der Vergangenheit im Verlauf war, als ein neues Ereignis eintrat.

7 **Eine Fahrt in die Stadt. Setze die Verben ins *simple past*.**

Yesterday Liz and her mother ____________ (go) into town. They ____________ (take) the bus. On their way they ____________ (see) a car accident. The policemen ____________ (be) already there.
Liz and her mother _________________ (get off) the bus in front of a big department store. They ____________ (buy) two T-shirts and a jacket for Liz.
On their way home, they ____________ (stop) at a supermarket. They ____________ (go) in and ____________ (get) potatoes and lettuce for dinner. Then they ____________ (walk) home and ____________ (have) dinner with the whole family.

8 **Übersetze die folgenden Sätze. Schreibe sie in dein Übungsheft.**

a) Tom und Tina waren glücklich.
b) Meine Familie hatte einen großen Hund.
c) Es war nicht sehr lustig.
d) Gestern waren wir zu Hause.
e) Er hatte eine Erkältung.
f) Letzten Montag war ich krank.
g) Letzten Sommer arbeitete Frank nicht im Zoo.
h) Es war ein kalter Morgen.

9 **Fülle die Lücken mit der richtigen Zeitform – *past progressive* oder *simple past?***

a) I ____________________ (eat) a sandwich when the phone ________________ (ring).

b) When Tina ________________ (enter) the restaurant, her family ____________________ (wait) there.

c) While they ____________________ (sit) in the waiting room, the door ________________ (open) and an old lady ________________ (come) in.

d) Mum ________________ (come) home while I ________________ ________________ (play) with our dog.

e) Ryan ____________________ (do) his homework when Mr Miller ________________ (call).

10 ***Simple past*** **oder** ***past progressive?***

a) We ______________________ (meet) our friends from California a few years ago while they ______________________ (visit) Europe.

b) Before she ______________________ (go) out to dinner, she ______________________ (take) a shower, ______________________ (paint) her fingernails and ______________________ (dress) nicely.

c) Shakespeare ______________________ (write) many theatre plays.

d) Mum ______________________ (want) to know: "What ______________________ (you/do) at 11 p.m. last night? You look awfully tired! What time ______________________ (you/get home) from the party last night?"

e) When I ______________________ (look) out of the window last Christmas morning, it ______________________ (snow).

f) As a girl, I ______________________ (play) the flute.

g) I ______________________ (watch) TV when I suddenly ______________________ (notice) a strange smell.

11 **Formuliere Fragen nach dem farbig markierten Satzglied. Schreibe in dein Übungsheft.**

a) Steve broke his arm fooling around in school two weeks ago.
b) Laura met her friends in the shopping mall.
c) Mum was preparing lunch when the postman rang.
d) Sarah wrote a letter to her boyfriend.
e) Last summer, Lily rode her bike to school every day.

7.-8. KLASSE

12 ***Simple past* oder *past progressive?* Höre dir Track 3 auf der CD an und setze die richtigen Formen ein.** 3

Last summer, I ______________ a frightening experience. At that time I ____________________________ in the USA. I ______________ my tent quite regularly in one of the many national parks, and I always ______________ very well. One night, however, while I ____________ ______________ a book in the flickering light of my torch, I ______________ somebody scream. I ______________ my book and ______________ my flashlight off. I __________________________ my shoes when I ______________ a terrible snort. Something enormous ___________________________ in front of my tent! I ______________________ to breathe. "That might be a bear," I ______________. Then I ___________________ my whistle. I ______________ the whistle and the bear _________________. I _________________ when I ___________________ my flashlight on again and I ______________________________ well that night. Next morning, when I ______________ into the next village to do some shopping, I ______________ a ranger about bears in national parks. He ______________ me that there had been no bear around at all the previous night. I ______________ again: __________________________ a dream when I ______________ the screaming and snorting the night before? I ______________________, but I ____________________ to stay in motels for the rest of my holidays.

4.3 Das *present perfect*

Present perfect simple* und *progressive

Das ***present perfect simple*** wird mit *have/has + past participle* (regelmäßig und unregelmäßig) gebildet: *I have loved, she has written.* Es wird verwendet, wenn ein Ereignis in der Vergangenheit begonnen hat und in die Gegenwart hinein andauert oder Folgen in der oder für die Gegenwart hat. Signalwörter: *already, never, before, (not) yet, since, for.*

Das ***present perfect progressive,*** gebildet mit *have/has + been + -ing-Form (I have been reading),* wird verwendet, wenn eine Handlung in der Vergangenheit begonnen hat und in die Gegenwart hinein andauert sowie um die Dauer der Handlung zu betonen. Signalwörter: *how long ...?, all day/week, for hours.*

13 **Setze das *present perfect* ein.**

a) Ida's bike is shining. She _______ just ___________ (clean) it.

b) ________ you ____________ (do) your homework? – Yes, I ________ already _______________ (finish) it.

c) Jim _________________________ (must/take) his medicine.

d) Marc ____________________ (live) in Berlin for three years now.

e) We _______________________ (not/be) to France yet.

14 **Achte auf die Satzstellung der Signalwörter und bilde einen passenden Satz im *present perfect*. Schreibe in dein Übungsheft.**

just: Gina/to write/a letter
never: I/to listen/to Indian music
for: Harry and Kim/to work/in a restaurant/nine months
already: we/can *(können)* book our trip/to Paris
not yet: He/can *(dürfen)* go/to London

15 **Bilde Sätze im *present perfect* und entscheide, ob du *since* oder *for* benötigst. Schreibe in dein Übungsheft.**

I/to eat/Chinese food/I was 10 years old since
Julia and Ron/to know/each other/2006 since
the girls/to talk/on the phone/three hours for

16 **Familie Green und Familie Sanders wollen gemeinsam in Urlaub fahren. Setze in die Lücken die richtige Form des *present perfect* ein.**

Gina Green: "Mum, dad, wake up! We ______________________________ (oversleep). I ______________________________ (hear/not) the alarm clock. Lisa ______________________ (just/call). The Sanders __________ already ______________ (leave)."

(half an hour later)

Dad: " I ________________________ (prepare) the picnic. __________ you ______________ (take) a shower, Gina?"

Gina: "Yes, I _____________________________ (just/finish) in the bathroom. It's your turn now. __________ you ______________ (pack) some biscuits and a bottle of water?"

Dad: "Yes, I ________________ (put) everything in the bag. But I _________________________ (find/not) our swimsuits."

Mum: "I _______________________ (just/see) them on the table over there."

Gina: "Listen, the phone is ringing! ... Lisa ________________________ (call) again. The Sanders _______________________ (turn) back home because they __________________________ (forget) their money."

17 **Nur eine Antwort ist richtig. Kreuze die Lösung an und trage sie ein.**

a) Your dress looks beautiful, __________ just ____________ it?

- [ ] did you buy
- [x] have you bought
- [ ] had you buy

b) Have you ever ________________ to San Francisco?

- [ ] were
- [x] been
- [ ] seen

c) My new car is a Porsche. I ____________________ of having a fast car.

- [ ] had always dreamt
- [ ] had been dreaming
- [x] have always dreamt

d) The window is broken. He _________________ it with his ball.

- [x] has just smashed
- [ ] smashed
- [ ] were smashing

e) I'm tired. It is really hot and I ______________________ all day, but I agreed to paint the house completely.

- [ ] was working
- [x] have been working
- [ ] worked

f) It's 11 a.m. already. How long ________________________?

- [ ] slept the baby
- [x] has the baby been sleeping
- [ ] was the baby sleeping

18 **Dein/e Austauschschüler/-in ist zu Besuch. Stelle ihm/ihr Fragen und schreibe sie in dein Übungsheft. Überlege, ob du *simple past* oder *present perfect* verwenden musst, wenn du fragst, ob er/sie …**

… letzte Nacht gut geschlafen hat.
… mit dem Zug nach Deutschland gekommen ist.
… schon einmal in Deutschland gewesen ist.
… schon einmal deutsche Gummibärchen *(jelly babies)* gegessen hat.

Did you sleep well last night?
" " come to Germany by train?
Have you ever been to Germany?
Have you ever eaten German jelly babies?

8.-10. KLASSE

since und for

Since bezeichnet den Zeitpunkt, zu dem eine Handlung einsetzt: *I have had this job since 2006.*
For bezeichnet eine Zeitspanne oder die Dauer eines Geschehens oder einer Handlung: *I have had this job for three years.*

19 **Formuliere die Sätze um, indem du *for* oder *since* benutzt. Schreibe in dein Übungsheft.**
Beispiel: *Sara lives in California. She arrived there two years ago.* → *Sara has been living in California for two years.*

a) Jim plays the piano. He started it when she was six years old. has been playing the piano started
b) We prepare a dinner party. We started to prepare it at 4 p.m.
c) My dad has got an old computer. He bought it in 1990.
d) Amy and Evan own a house. They bought it six years ago.

We have been preparing a dinner party

20 **Ergänze die Sätze mit *for* oder *since* und setze das Verb in den Klammern in die richtige Form: *present perfect simple* oder *progressive?***

a) We ____________________ (wait) for the painters __________ the beginning of the week.

b) The men ____________________ (work) __________ hours, and they're tired now.

c) Jane _________________ (improve) her English __________ the summer holidays.

d) Jessica seems to be away. I ____________________ (try) to contact her a week now.

e) Jenny ______________________ (send) me a postcard every week __________ she _____________ (be) in Rome.

4.4 Das *past perfect*

Past *perfect simple* und *progressive*

Das ***past perfect simple*** wird gebildet aus *had + past participle: I had looked, we had seen.* Es wird verwendet, wenn man sich auf einen Zeitpunkt bezieht, der sich vor einem Ereignis im *simple past* ereignet hat (Vorvergangenheit). Das ***past perfect progressive,*** gebildet aus *had + been + -ing*-Form *(I had been watching)* drückt aus, dass eine Handlung in der Vergangenheit andauerte, als ein anderes Ereignis einsetzte.

21 **Vervollständige die folgenden Sätze mit der *past perfect simple*-Form des Verbs in Klammern.**

a) After we ________________ (buy) the tickets, we went to the hall.

b) I phoned the police because someone ____________________ (steal) my car.

c) John ________________________ (not/finish) his homework when Peter phoned.

d) ____________ you ____________ (go) to Bristol before you flew to Rome?

22 **Mache aus zwei eins: Verbinde die einzelnen Sätze in der angegebenen Reihenfolge mit *after, when* oder *before.* Schreibe in dein Übungsheft.**
Beispiel: *Her parents sold their house.* (2) *They bought a bungalow.* (1) → *After her parents had sold the house, they bought a bungalow.*

a) Ben left school (1). He went to university (2).
b) The lessons began (2). The pupils got to school (1).
c) The train left (1). They got to the station (2).
d) The thieves left the bank (1). The police arrived (2).
e) I started breakfast (1). The doorbell rang (2).

23 **Sarah und Sam wollen heiraten. Schreibe vollständige Sätze mit dem *past perfect simple* in dein Übungsheft. Beginne jeden Satz mit *after*.**

Sarah and Sam / decide to marry / send out invitation cards
they / send out invitation cards / look around for a nice party location
they / decide on a meal / go shopping for a wedding dress and a suit
they / have everything ready / Sam and Sarah / panic: the idea of having such a big party was simply too much for them.
they / say sorry to all their friends / the two of them / fly to the Caribbean Sea
they / get married / on the beach of a romantic island / have a wonderful honeymoon

24 **Lies die folgende Geschichte durch und markiere alle Verben. Erzähle dann die Geschichte absatzweise rückwärts, indem du das *past perfect* benutzt. Schreibe in dein Übungsheft.**

Yesterday, Evan got up early and took his kids to the zoo. Maya enjoyed watching the penguins, and Milo had a lot of fun feeding the ducks. After a picnic lunch, Evan bought the kids an ice cream. Maya and Milo were running around the zoo for many hours and had a perfect day. At home, Evan's wife Amy had a wonderful day, too. She enjoyed the quietness. She took a bath. She read a book and took a nap *(Nickerchen)* in the sunshine. And after so many hours to herself, she was looking forward to seeing her family again.

→ Yesterday, after many hours to herself,
Amy was looking forward to seeing her family
again. She had had a wonderful ...

25 **Sam erzählt seinem Freund am Telefon, wie das Robbie-Williams-Konzert am Abend zuvor war. Wähle die richtige Form: *past perfect simple* oder *progressive?***

"… Well, I went with Emma. You know Emma, don't you? She is gorgeous! Anyway, when we were getting on the bus to go to the concert, I realized that I ____________________ (forget) my money. So we both got off again. I didn't want to miss the concert because I ____________________________ (look forward to) it for a few weeks. So we ran, but when we got to my house, I realized that I ______________________ (not/take) a key with me either, so I couldn't get in. Unfortunately, no one was at home because everybody _________________ (go) out. So we decided to go to Emma's instead. Before her granny opened the door, we _________________________ (ring) the doorbell for about 15 minutes. Just imagine – her granny is almost deaf! Luckily she gave us a few quid, and we rushed back to the bus stop, but before we got there the bus ___________ ____________________ (already/leave).

Well, to cut it short – when we finally made it to the concert, we couldn't get in because the concert ____________________________ (already/begin) – but Emma was worth all the trouble and money I ____________________ (spend) on the ticket …"

4.5 Das *future*

Die verschiedenen Futurarten

Zukünftige Ereignisse und Handlungen können im Englischen mithilfe unterschiedlicher Zeitformen formuliert werden. Bei den Futurformen unterscheidet man

- das ***going to-future:*** *be* + *going to* + Infinitiv: *I am going to eat,*
- das ***will-future:*** *will* + Infinitiv: *I will eat* (Kurzform verneint: *won't),*
- das ***future progressive:*** *will* + *be* + *-ing*-Form: *I will be eating,*
- das ***future perfect:*** *will* + *have* + *past participle: I will have eaten.*

Welches Futur zum Einsatz kommt, hängt von der Perspektive ab.

26 **Spontane Entscheidung *(will-future)* oder fester Vorsatz *(going to-future)*? Setze die passende Zukunftsform ein.**

Ray: "Look here, my bike. I can't use it, the brakes are not working. My dad __________________ (repair) it on Saturday."

Simon: "Don't wait until Saturday. I __________________ (check) it for you."

Ray: "Thanks, but I need new brakes. Dad and I __________________ ________ (buy) them on Saturday. Do you want to come with us?"

Simon: "Yes, of course, I __________________ (come), too."

Ray: "And what about next Friday? I ____________________________ (play) basketball with Tom and Jerry."

Simon: "I can't. Diana is in hospital, and I __________________________ (visit) her next Friday."

27 **Am letzten Schultag vor den Ferien unterhalten sich die Schüler und Schülerinnen über ihre Pläne. Verwende die passenden Formen des Futurs, um die Sätze zu vervollständigen.**

Michael: "I ______________________ (not/study) any vocabulary over the holidays. However, I ______________________ (stay) with my girlfriend at her aunt for one week. And as soon as I ______________________ (finish) school next summer, I ________________ (take) her on a trip round the world."

Sarah: "I hope it ______________ (be) hot all summer. Then I ______________________ (spend) all afternoons at the swimming-pool. I assume I ________________ (get) a good tan *(Sonnenbräune)* then."

Mary: "I ______________________ (sleep in) all the days. And I ______________________ (do) a lot of shopping around in our shopping-centre."

Susie: "My parents and I ______________________ (spend) two weeks in Greece. I guess we ________________ (do) a lot of sight-seeing there."

Sharif: "I ________________ (redecorate) my room. Maybe I ________________ (make) a new shelf. I hope I ________________ ________________ (finish) the work until school starts again."

Monica: "We ________________________ (host) an exchange student from New Zealand. She ________________________ (arrive) at London Airport next Saturday. And I ________________________ (visit) her in New Zealand over Christmas."

Marc: "I ________________ (not/do) anything special. I ______________ ______________________ (just relax and see) what happens."

28 **Verwende das *future perfect*.**

a) Next year, my husband and I ___________________________ (be married) for ten long and endless years.

b) Don't worry. The plane ____________________________ (not/leave) before we get to the airport.

c) Next summer I _____________________________ (work) in the same boring job with the same company for over eight years.

29 **Übersetze die folgenden Sätze ins Englische. Achte auf die richtige Zukunftsform und schreibe die Sätze in dein Übungsheft!**

a) Unser Zug fährt in 20 Minuten. Wann kommen wir in New Orleans an?
b) Nächste Woche fliegen wir nach Denver und werden dort zwei Wochen bleiben.
c) Michael wird im Urlaub gelernt haben, wie man surft.
d) Wenn er 70 ist, wird er immer noch herumrennen.
e) Wenn du ankommst, werden meine Eltern auf dich warten.
f) Der Mechaniker wird die Geschirrspülmaschine bis Montag nicht repariert haben.

30 **Entscheide dich für die richtige Zeitform: *will-future* oder *future perfect?* Streiche die falsche Form durch.**

a) When will you have finished/will you finish your project on Native Americans?

b) I think we will have had/will have hot weather in Florida.

c) Mum, by the time you get home, I will do/will have done the washing up. I promise.

d) Don't worry! Dad is a careful driver – I'm sure he will come/will have come soon.

e) By this time next year, Bob will leave/will have left university.

f) I suppose Jamie will have been/will be late again.

31 **In dieser Übung werden alle Zeitformen des Futurs getestet. Finde die Fehler in den folgenden Sätzen und schreibe die richtigen Sätze in dein Übungsheft. Vorsicht: Nicht alle Sätze sind falsch!**

a) You can't carry all those bags. Just a moment. I'm helping you.
b) Will you do anything tomorrow evening?
c) Why have you put on those old clothes? I will paint the fence.
d) What time will the last bus leave? I must catch it.
e) Hasn't the doorbell just rung? I'll go.
f) Tom is sure that he is going to pass his final exams.
g) The Queen is visiting Ascot as in the years before.
h) By the time we arrive, she will make all the sandwiches.
i) Geoffrey will be sixty next June.
j) It is possibly going to be another boring weekend.

5

Das Passiv

5.1 Das Passiv im *present tense*

Das Passiv im *simple present* und *present progressive*

Das Passiv *(passive voice)* stellt eine Handlung aus einer anderen Sicht dar: In einem **Aktivsatz** führt das Subjekt eine Handlung aus: *A policeman* ***stops*** *the traffic every morning*. In einem **Passivsatz** geschieht etwas mit dem Subjekt: *The traffic* ***is stopped*** *every morning*.
Das Passiv im ***simple present*** wird gebildet mit *is/are + past participle: A letter is written every day.*
Das Passiv im ***present progressive*** wird gebildet mit *is/are being + past participle: A letter is being written at the moment.*

1 **Vervollständige die folgenden Sätze mit der korrekten Passivform. Achte auf die richtige Zeit: *present simple* oder *progressive?***

a) In Switzerland four languages ________________ (speak).

b) Do you know when the post ________________________ (usually/collect)?

c) Look, Kevin! Your bed ____________________ (make) again.

d) The bins ________________ (always/empty) in the evening.
It is 6 p.m. – the bins ____________________ (empty) now.

e) A lot of apples and pears ________________ (grow) here.

f) The grass ________________ (cut) at the moment.

7. KLASSE

Das persönliche Passiv

Das persönliche Passiv *(personal passive)* ist nur bei Verben mit zwei Objekten möglich. Es liegt dann vor, wenn das indirekte Objekt des Aktivsatzes eine Person ist, die zum **Subjekt des Passivsatzes** gemacht werden soll: *The school gave the students their reports.* → ***The students were given** their reports. They showed us a lot of interesting things.* → ***We were shown** a lot of interesting things* („Man zeigte uns ...“).

2 **Finde zu den folgenden Passivsätzen die zweite Möglichkeit, um das Passiv mit zwei Objekten zu bilden. Schreibe die Sätze in dein Übungsheft.**
Beispiel: ***Our dog is usually given a dog biscuit in the evening.* → *A dog biscuit is usually given to our dog in the evening.***

a) The guests are just being offered coffee.
b) I am often told silly stories.
c) Every lesson new English exercises are given to us.
d) They are being told some important information.
e) A new bike is usually promised Pete before his birthday.

3 **Setze die folgenden Sätze ins Passiv.**
Beispiel: ***My parents give me my pocket money every month.* → *I am given my pocket money by my ...***

a) Tim never tells us funny jokes.

____

b) The guide is showing the tourists the most interesting sights.

____

c) John's friends never offer him a cigarette.

____

d) Every summer Pat sends her penfriend a long letter.

____

4 **Finde die Fehler in den folgenden Sätzen und verbessere sie.**

a) Us are told very interesting facts in our history lesson.

____

b) Sandwiches are often given him for dinner.

____

c) The leaflets send to the tourists every spring.

____

5 **Verwandle die Sätze vom Aktiv ins Passiv. Aufgepasst: Manchmal gibt es zwei Möglichkeiten.**

a) The teacher explains the problems to the pupils.

____

____

____________________ /

____

____

b) This shop accepts credit cards.

____

c) Mum allowed Laura to go to the party.

____

d) John gave Lisa a bracelet for Christmas.

____ /

____

Das Passiv bei Verben des Sagens und Meinens

Verben des Sagens und Meinens bzw. Denkens bilden das Passiv, indem man *to* + Vollverb an die Passivkonstruktion anhängt: *Jim **is said to be** a liar* („**Man sagt,** Jim ist ein Lügner").
Wenn eine Information nicht unbedingt gesichert ist, kann man eine Konstruktion mit *it,* einer Form von *be,* dem *past participle* und *that* verwenden: ***It is said/reported that** the President has fallen ill* („Es heißt/wird berichtet, der Präsident sei krank geworden").

6 **Übersetze und schreibe in dein Übungsheft.**

Man sagt, er sei sehr reich.
Es wird berichtet, dass bei dem Unfall vier Menschen getötet wurden.
Man behauptet von Susie, sie sei eine gute Schülerin.
Es wird angenommen *(to think),* dass der Präsident morgen eine Rede hält.

4

7 **Höre dir Track 4 auf der CD an und vervollständige die Sätze mit einem Verb des Sagens oder Meinens im Passiv.**

a) Tom ____________________ very sensitive.

b) The president didn't appear for the talk show. ____________________ __________ that he couldn't come because he is quite ill.

c) Thousands of children ____________________ to have lost a close relative in the earthquake in Asia in 2004.

d) Last night, a serious accident happened on the motorway to London. ____________________________ four people were killed.

e) Angelina Jolie ____________________ to be pregnant again.

Modalverben im Passiv

Wird ein Satz, in dem ein modales Hilfsverb steht, im Passiv verwendet, bleibt **das modale Hilfsverb** des Aktivsatzes (*can, must* usw.) oder die entsprechende Ersatzform (*to have to, to be able to, to be allowed to* usw.) **unverändert.** Nur das Vollverb nimmt die Passivform an. Aktiv: *You must/have to* ***carry*** *your suitcase to the station.* Passiv: *Your suitcase must/has to* ***be carried*** *to the station.*

8 **Verwandle die Sätze vom Aktiv ins Passiv.**

A football game

The team must follow the rules.

____

____

All members of the team have to wear their team shirt.

____

____

The goalkeeper ought to keep the goal clear.

____

____

The defender must stop the other team from scoring.

____

____

9 **Setze folgende Sätze mit Modalverben ins Passiv. Schreibe sie in dein Übungsheft.**

a) You must keep this door shut.
b) They should forbid this film.
c) Somebody must repair Helen's bike.
d) The President might open the new bridge tomorrow.

5.2 Das Passiv im *past tense*

Das Passiv im *simple past* und *past progressive*

Im ***simple past*** lauten die Formen des Passivs: *were/was + past participle: The boat was destroyed in the storm.*
Im ***past progressive*** lauten die Passivformen: *was/were being + past participle: I was being asked to go to the bank when the telephone rang.*

10 **Anne berichtet ihrem Tagebuch von ihren ersten Tagen in London, wohin sie umgezogen ist. Setze die richtigen Passivformen im *simple past* ein.**

Dear Diary,

Let me tell you about my new school. I ____________________ (welcome/warmly) by my new classmates. First, I ____________________ (show) our new classroom. Then, during my first week, a girl showed me around the neighbourhood. I ____________________ (teach) some history of the city, too. And I ____________________ (offer) to join my new school's volleyball team. I ____________________ (accept/quickly) by the teachers, too. I ____________________ (ask) a lot of questions.

My little sister is quite happy here, too. She, too, ____________________ (invite) to join her school's sports team. However, we ____________________ (tell) by our neighbours that we have to close all the windows each time she practises the piano. But last Saturday, we ____________________ (invite) to a big party by our new neighbours.

Der *by-agent*

Der Verursacher einer Handlung wird durch den *by-agent* genannt. Er entspricht dem Subjekt des Aktivsatzes: ***Alan's dog** has just bitten the postman.* → *The postman has just been bitten* **by Alan's dog.**
Er steht meistens am Ende des Satzes und kann weggelassen werden, wenn er unwichtig oder offensichtlich ist: *The bank was robbed (by robbers).*

11 **Setze folgende Sätze ins Passiv. Einige der Sätze benötigen einen *by-agent*. Schreibe sie in dein Übungsheft.**

a) The dustmen collect rubbish.
b) Everyone had finished the job at seven.
c) They have sold the house.
d) The police warned you.
e) David Beckham scored the winning goal.
f) Someone is showing the film now.
g) Somebody has stolen Bob's bike.
h) People always admire him.

12 **Verfasse aus den folgenden Satzteilen einen Unfallbericht. Benutze das Passiv dort, wo es sinnvoll ist, und achte auf die richtige Zeit. Denke auch an den *by-agent*.**

accident – to happen – between Bath and Bristol – yesterday // one crash victim – to take – to hospital – an ambulance // an injured woman – to pull from a burning car – passing motorists – but the driver – not to rescue // passenger in the Mercedes – to take to hospital – he – to keep under observation – at the moment // the police believe – the driver of the Mercedes – to lose control on the wet road // witnesses – to interview – police – at present // motorway – to open again – recently // since this terrible accident – motorists – to drive – more carefully

13 **Setze die richtige Form im *past progressive* in die Lücken.**

a) The wallpaper ______________________________ (take down) when the phone rang.

b) A party ______________________________ (hold) when a heavy thunderstorm struck.

c) Exams ______________________ (write) when the fire alarm set off.

d) When I came home from school last week, our car ______________ ____________________ (haul away).

14 **Verbinde die Satzteile in den Kästen miteinander und bilde mit ihnen das persönliche Passiv im *simple past*. Schreibe sie in dein Übungsheft und übersetze die Sätze anschließend ins Deutsche.**

Our teachers allowed	us some useful information about NYC.
They advised	us to be careful.
They promised	us to visit Manhattan.
They told	us to book the trip through a travel agency.
They gave	us to organize a trip to New York.

5.3 Das Passiv im *present perfect* und *past perfect*

Das Passiv im *present perfect* und *past perfect*

Die Passivformen im ***present perfect*** werden gebildet mit *has been/have been* sowie dem *past participle* des Vollverbs: *A story has been written.*
Im ***past perfect*** wird das Passiv mit *had been* und dem *past participle* gebildet: *Even though Kate had been promised a horse she didn't get one for her birthday.*
Die *progressive*-Formen werden nur sehr selten verwendet: *My bike has/had been being stolen.*

15 **Wandle die Verben ins Passiv um.**

have taught → ____________________

has taken → ____________________

had sung → ____________________

has treated → ____________________

had kept → ____________________

have put → ____________________

had drunk → ____________________

have seen → ____________________

had painted → ____________________

16 **Höre dir Track 5 auf der CD an. Dort werden einzelne Aktivsätze vorgelesen. Schreibe sie auf und verwandle die Sätze dann ins Passiv. Achtung: Bei zwei Sätzen gibt es zwei verschiedene Möglichkeiten! Schreibe die Sätze in dein Übungsheft.**

5

17 **Gemischte Passivzeiten. Beschreibe, was im Haus der Reynolds passiert ist, als sie im Urlaub waren. Benutze das Passiv und achte auf die Stellung der Präpositionen. Manchmal ist es sinnvoll, den *by-agent* zu verwenden. Beginne so: *While the Reynolds were on holiday, ...***

while/the Reynolds/on holiday – their house/to break into/two burglars

after/the windows/to break – the living room/to enter

a lot of valuable objects/to take

before/the diamonds/to steal – the door of the safe/to open

the police/to call/by Mrs Marble – while/the house/to clear out

while/the house/to leave – the burglars/to arrest/by the police

18 **Aktiv oder Passiv? Entscheide dich für die richtige Zeitform des Verbs in Klammern. Vergiss nicht, die richtige Zeit zu benutzen.**

Yesterday a 32-year-old swimmer ______________________ (kill) by a shark in Australia. This terrible accident ______________________ (happen) near the city of Perth. The lifeguards tried their best to save the swimmer, but after he ______________________ (pull) out of the water, the heavily injured man ______________________ (die). A friend, who ______________________ (drag) the victim to the shore, ______________________ (bite) on his legs and feet and ______________________ (must/take) to hospital.
Since last September three men ______________________ (become) victims of sharks in Australia. Among others, a 23-year-old surfer ______________ (pull) from his surfboard before the tourists ____________________ (warn) about the sharks. Some tourists ______________ (find) his board, but his body ______________________ (disappear) without a trace.
Only a few days later, a tourist from England, _____________________ (attack) by a shark. Luckily, the young man from Derbyshire, England, ______________________ (survive). However, he ___________________ (treat) in hospital now. He ______________________ (suppose) to fly back to England by the end of next week. Shark attacks are very unusual.
It ____________________________ (investigate) what is causing the aggressive behaviour of the sharks.

5.4 Das Passiv im *will-future*

Das Passiv mit *will*

Auch das ***will-future*** kann eine Passivform bilden. Sie wird gebildet mithilfe von *will be* sowie dem *past participle: The new car model will be released in May.*
Ebenfalls kann das ***future perfect*** ins Passiv gesetzt werden mit *will have been + past participle: The TV will have been repaired by this evening.*

19 **Mary schenkt ihrer Freundin Susie ein Hundebaby. Susie sagt ihrem neuen Hund, was geschehen wird. Schreibe die Sätze in dein Übungsheft.**
Beispiel: *regular walks/take out → You will be taken out for regular walks.*

plenty of water and food/give – I treat you well – regular check-ups at the vet's/take – extra treats once in a while/give – all family members/love you

20 **Setze die richtige *future perfect*-Form im Passiv ein.**

a) The project ____________________ (complete) before the deadline.

b) Don't worry about the weather: All things ____________________ (take) inside before the rain.

c) The film shooting is over. But the movie ____________________ (not/release) by next month.

21 **Vermischte Passivzeiten. In jedem Satz befindet sich ein Fehler. Verbessere die Sätze.**

a) To Jason was promised a better salary.

____

b) Her was thanked for her hard work.

____

c) About the environment will be talked in the weeks to come.

____

d) An enormous Valentine card has been sent my brother.

____

e) At Kim hasn't been shouted since she was a kid.

____

f) Rivers or lakes mustn't be use as dumping grounds for toxic waste.

____

22 **Höre dir Track 6 auf der CD an. Dort werden einzelne Sätze vorgelesen. Übersetze diese Sätze ins Deutsche. Schreibe in dein Übungsheft.**

6

6 Modale Hilfsverben

6.1 *Can* und *could*

Können/dürfen

Das modale Hilfsverb *can* wird durch die Formen ***can't/cannot*** verneint. Die Formen im *past tense* lauten ***could/couldn't.***
Ist eine Fähigkeit gemeint, wird *could* in den anderen Zeitformen durch die Ersatzform ***to be able to*** ersetzt: *I won't be able to repair my bike.*
Can/could bezeichnet eine allgemeine Fähigkeit, *to be able to* bezieht sich auf eine spezielle Situation.
Die Ersatzform für *can/could* zum Ausdruck einer Erlaubnis oder eines Verbots ist ***to be allowed to:*** *You are allowed to park your car over there.*
Could kann nicht nur „konnte", sondern auch „könnte" bedeuten: *We could go there by car, couldn't we?*

1 **Setze die passende Form in die Lücke: *can, could* oder Ersatzform? Manchmal gibt es zwei Möglichkeiten – trage beide ein. Achte auf die Zeiten.**

a) Last year we ____________________________ go to India.

b) Oh dear! I can't do this translation. _________________________ you help me with that translation?

c) At the moment Marc _________________________ (not) play the bass. But next year he _______________________ *(will-future)* play the bass.

d) Toby ___________________________ (not) ride a bike when he was three. Now he's ten, so he _________________________ ride a bike.

e) _________________________ climb Mount Everest?

f) _________________________ you speak louder, please?

6. KLASSE

2 **Setze die fehlenden Formen von *to be allowed to* ein. Achte auf die richtige Zeitform.**

a) You ____________________ (not) turn left, but you ____________________ turn right.

b) She ____________________ (not) borrow the skateboard last week.

c) ____________________ (you) watch TV last week?

d) Dogs ____________________ (not) in the cinema.

3 **Benutze die modalen Hilfsverben und die entsprechenden Ersatzformen, um die nachfolgenden Sätze umzuformulieren. Ergänze nach jedem Satz, welche Funktion das Hilfsverb hat.**
Beispiel: ***It sometimes gets very cold here in the winter.*** **⟶** ***It can get very cold here in the winter. (Möglichkeit)***

a) The shop assistant didn't know a word of English.

____

____

b) Perhaps the shops on Queens Road are still open – it's just possible.

____

____

c) It's not possible to sit at this table. It's reserved.

____

____

d) Come in, Mrs Collins!

____

____

6.2 *Must, needn't* und *mustn't*

Müssen, nicht brauchen **und** ***nicht dürfen***

Must kannst du nur in der Gegenwart verwenden. Für die anderen Zeiten brauchst du die **Ersatzform *to have (got) to.*** Das *got* wird nur im *simple present* benötigt: *I must tidy my room today.* → *I had to tidy my room yesterday.*
Must wird mit ***needn't*** verneint: *I must go to school, but I needn't go to the sports club.* In anderen Zeiten als dem Präsens benutzt du ***not to have to:***
I didn't have to tidy my room yesterday.
Zwischen *must* und *to have got to* gibt es einen Bedeutungsunterschied: *Must* drückt ein persönliches Bedürfnis aus, *to have got to* bezeichnet einen äußeren Zwang.
Achtung: ***Mustn't*** bedeutet *nicht dürfen: You mustn't eat all the cookies.*

4 **Fülle die Lücken mit der passenden Form von *to have to.* Achte auf die Signalwörter für die Vergangenheit und für das *will-future!* An zwei Stellen musst du eine Frage formulieren.**

A three-day snowboard course

Instructor: "Good morning everyone. How do you feel after your first day of snowboarding?"

Betty: "I feel good today but I ________________ go to bed early yesterday. I was so tired."

Instructor: "That's alright. Yesterday you ________________ learn all the basics (*Grundlagen*). Today we will practise *(üben)* a lot. Remember, tomorrow you ________________ pass a test. So we ________________ start right away *(sofort)*."

John: "Can we put on our snowboards right now? Or __________ __________ have a warming-up first?"

Instructor: "Of course you always ________________ do a warming-up first. Today you ________________ get up the hill with the lift.

To use the lift – what ________________ do?"

Steven: "We ______________ stand on the snowboard with one foot only."

Instructor: "Right. Good luck – I will see you on top of the hill."

5 **Achte auf den Bedeutungsunterschied: *must* (persönliches Bedürfnis) oder *to have to* (äußerer Zwang)?**

a) My teacher is very strict. I _____________do my homework.

b) I was running for one hour. I ____________ drink something.

c) *Mother to Jill:* "Don't be late! You _____________ be home at 10 o'clock!" – *Jill to her friends:* "I _____________ be home at 10. My mother told me so."

6 **Überlege, ob du *mustn't, needn't* oder *don't have to* einsetzen musst. Übersetze nur die roten Satzteile. Schreibe sie in dein Übungsheft.**

a) Du musst nicht in die Schule gehen.

b) Du brauchst mir nicht zu helfen, ich komme allein zurecht.

c) Du darfst nicht zu viel trinken, du bekommst sonst Bauchweh.

d) Ihr braucht nicht zu bezahlen, ich lade euch ein.

e) Du musst heute nicht früh ins Bett gehen.

f) Ich darf heute nicht lange aufbleiben *(stay up)*.

6.3 *Shall, should* und *ought to*

Sollen und _sollten_

Shall wird verwendet, um einen Wunsch zu erfragen oder einen Vorschlag zu machen: *Shall we have lunch now?*
Should/shouldn't wird verwendet, um einen Ratschlag zu erteilen, eine Verpflichtung zum Ausdruck zu bringen oder eine begründete Vermutung zu äußern: *You shouldn't drive so fast here. Pete should to be here soon.*
Ought to ist gleichbedeutend mit *should: You ought to read more.*

7 **Formuliere die folgenden Vorschläge in deinem Übungsheft mit *shall* um.**
Beispiel: *Let's go for a walk.* → *Shall we go for a walk?*

a) I can open the window.
b) Let's have something to eat.
c) Let's have a break.
d) I can aswer the phone.

8 **Formuliere Ratschläge oder Verpflichtungen mit *should* oder *shouldn't*.**

a) It's late. I think we ______________________________ (go home).

b) These shoes are too big for you. I don't think you ________________ ________________ (buy them).

c) This car is too expensive. I think Mr Hill ______________________ ________________ (look for a cheaper one).

d) You look terrible. Aren't you well this morning? I think you __________ ________________ (go to work).

e) James has put on weight. The doctor thinks he __________________ ________________ (eat too much).

9 **Übersetze die folgenden Sätze ins Englische und achte besonders auf die richtige Übersetzung von *müssen* und *sollen!* Schreibe in dein Übungsheft.**

a) Mein Fahrrad ist schmutzig. Ich muss es putzen.
b) Wo sollen wir dieses Jahr Urlaub machen?
c) Du solltest mehr Sport machen.
d) Sollen wir uns um 19.30 Uhr treffen?
e) Musst du früh ins Bett?
f) Musstet ihr gestern lange vor dem Kino warten?

10 **Dein englischer Brieffreund besucht dich. Du unterhältst dich mit ihm über einen möglichen Ausflug. Benutze *shall/should/ought to.***

go hiking – in the nearby forest?:

____

perhaps – we – raincoats with us:

It looks like rain. ______________________________

we – walk not too far:

But ______________________________. It still gets dark quite early.

take sandwiches? – make them?:

____

have a picnic – by the lakeside?:

____

take a blanket to sit on:

____

get up not too late:

If we want to go hiking, ______________________________

6.4 *May* und *might*

Dürfte/könnte

May und *might* werden verwendet, um **Möglichkeiten** oder **Wahrscheinlichkeiten** auszudrücken: *He may be right. Nick might be still asleep.* Man kann mit *may* und *might* auch um **Erlaubnis** bitten oder ein **Verbot** formulieren (förmlicher als mit *to be allowed to*): *Might we borrow your car for tonight? You may not smoke in here.*

11 **Was könntest du in den folgenden Situationen sagen? Wähle das richtige Hilfsverb, um eine Möglichkeit, Wahrscheinlichkeit oder Erlaubnis zum Ausdruck zu bringen.**

a) It's cold outside and has started to rain. Be careful when you cycle home. The roads ______________________________.

b) Caroline __________________________. I'll phone her and see.

c) I want to invite some people to my party on Friday. ________________ Kevin, too.

d) In August I will have some days off. ______________________ ______________ in Ireland.

e) I must phone my parents because I'm late again. _____________ __________________?

f) I like your new bike. __________________________________?

g) I think Judy will be 18 next month. But I ___________________ __________________.

6.5 *Will* und *would*

Wird und würde

Mit ***will*** (Verneinung ***won't***) formuliert man Bitten, Einladungen oder Angebote, Befehle, Annahmen, Wahrscheinlichkeiten oder ein typisches Verhalten: *Will you please pass me the milk? Ray will be in Seattle by now. That'll be the milkman, I'm sure. On holiday Janet will write letters for hours* („pflegt ... zu schreiben").

Would (Verneinung ***wouldn't***) wird wie *will* gebraucht, ist jedoch höflicher. Es kann eine Bitte, eine Einladung oder ein Angebot ausdrücken: *I would like to meet you again. What would you like to do?*

Auch eine Wahrscheinlichkeit oder ein typisches Verhalten in der Vergangenheit kann mit *would* formuliert werden: *At the weekends my friends would play tennis* („pflegten ... zu spielen").

12 **Benutze *will* oder *would*, um die Bitten und Einladungen zu den folgenden Sätzen zu formulieren. Die Wendungen aus dem Wortspeicher helfen dir dabei. Schreibe in dein Übungsheft.**

Beispiel: ***You have got a nasty cough all the time. Will/Would you see the doctor?***

dial for me – set the table – help me translate it – shut the window – go for a walk with the dog – have some more potatoes

a) I'm terribly busy in the kitchen, and I'm late anyway.

b) Jane, you can't just have peas and carrots.

c) It's getting quite cold in here.

d) I have no idea how your mobile phone works.

e) I've got this letter from that hotel in Spain.

f) Someone must take Bonzo for walk, but I'm not feeling my best today.

13 **Bilde aus den Satzteilen Wünsche, Wahrscheinlichkeiten oder Weigerungen. Benutze *will/won't* und *would/wouldn't*. Achte auf die richtigen Zeiten!**

a) Tracy – to go to Princeton – next year

____

____

b) Tracy's friend – not to study – to go abroad first

____

____

c) to tell me – your problem?

____

____

d) Brian – not to admit – he stole the money

____

____

14 **Vervollständige den Dialog mit *will/won't* und den angegebenen Verben.**

Martin: "Isn't that Pam's bike? I wonder what she's doing here at this time?"

Fiona: "I expect she ____________________ (be) at the newsagent's to buy some ciggies."

Martin: "You may be right. She ____________________ (want) to buy today's newspaper."

Judy: "Nonsense! I know Pam! She ____________________ (meet) her boyfriend Tom who lives above the newsagent's. That's for sure."

Martin: "Certainly. And they ____________________ (learn) German together."

Judy: "Well, they ____________________ (do) that – they have better things to do, but Pam ____________________ (smoke), I suppose."

Fiona: "Judy, you may be right, as ever. However, Pam ____________________ (lie) to me, you know. She hates Tom, she told me so!"

Martin: "Oh, be quiet. Look! Pam and Tom. Where are they going now?"

Fiona: "I don't care. I suppose Tom ____________________ (want) to have lunch at Pam's. Her mum ______________________________ (look forward to) meeting Tom, don't you think?"

15 Höre dir Track 7 auf der CD an und schreibe auf, was die Personen jeweils zu tun pflegen oder pflegten.

7

a) Some years ago, Steve ______________________________ in class.

b) Betty ______________________________ when she does her homework.

c) Mr Smith ______________________________ although his doctor told him several times to do so.

d) Years ago, Eddie ____ ____________________ for hours although his wife didn't like it.

e) When Sue was little, she ______________________________ whenever she heard music.

Die indirekte Rede

7.1 Die Veränderung der Pronomen

Der Standpunkt des Berichtenden

Mit der indirekten Rede *(reported speech)* gibt man wieder, was jemand sagt oder gesagt hat. Wie im Deutschen zeigt die indirekte Rede auch im Englischen den Standpunkt der Person, die berichtet. Die Pronomen werden dem Standpunkt des Berichtenden angepasst:
*Andy: "**I** can't help **you** with **your** homework, Jim." R Andy explains to Jim (that) **he** can't help **him** with **his** homework.*

1 **Gib wieder, was die folgenden Leute sagen.**

Boy: "I've lost my purse."

The boy says that ______________________________.

Girl: "I can't come to your party, Linda."

The girl tells Linda that ______________________________.

Parents: "We'll be home late."

My parents explain to me that ______________________________.

2 **Wandle die Sätze in der indirekten Rede in die direkte Rede um. Schreibe sie in dein Übungsheft.**
Beispiel: ***Lynn tells Richard that she is going to work in London. → Lynn to Richard: "I'm going to work in London."***

Sarah says she has forgotten to do her homework.
Mr Hall thinks that his children shouldn't go to parties.
His mother told Tim that he can't have a new computer.

7.2 Die Rückverschiebung der Zeiten

Regeln zur *backshift of tenses*

Steht das Verb des einleitenden Satzes im ***past tense*** oder ***past perfect,*** dann werden die Zeiten in der indirekten Rede um eine Zeitstufe gegenüber der direkten Rede zurück in die Vergangenheit verschoben: *Pete: "I **write** my penfriend every week." → Pete **said** that he **wrote** his penfriend every week.*
Dabei gilt:

- *present tense → past tense*
- *present progressive → past progressive*
- *present perfect → past perfect*
- *past tense → past perfect*
- *going-to future → was/were going to*
- *will-future → would + infinitive*
- *can → could; may → might*

3 **Wandle die Sätze, die gesagt werden, in die indirekte Rede um.**

Fiona: "I don't want to do anything."

Fiona said ____.

Beth: "My friend and I will probably visit some friends in Scotland."

Beth told me that ____.

Brian: "I have already spent my pocket money on comics."

Brian told us that ____.

Lucy: "I work at the supermarket every Saturday."

Lucy says ____.

Dave: "I may not be at home on Sunday."

Dave said ____.

Sophie: "I was ill on Wednesday."

Sophie told me that ______________________________________.

4 **Streiche die Fehler in den folgenden Sätzen an und verbessere sie.**

a) My cousin said he will meet me in front of the restaurant.

____

b) Richard told James that he is going to buy a new computer.

____

c) Mr Dixon said he hasn't been to a museum since 2001.

____

d) George told me that he can help with my English homework.

____

e) Tina said me that her parents had been strict when she was young.

____

5 **Übersetze die folgenden Sätze und schreibe sie in dein Übungsheft.**

a) Jane sagt, dass Mary gut in Biologie sei.
b) Mary sagte mir, dass sie später kommen werde.
c) Ann und Michael sagten, dass sie am Wochenende ins Kino gehen wollten.
d) Jenny sagt ihrer Mutter, dass sie einen Freund eingeladen hat.
e) Tom sagte, dass er 2005 angefangen hat, Gitarre zu spielen.

Say oder *tell?*

Auf ***say*** kann ein indirektes Objekt (Personenobjekt) folgen. Es muss dann **mit *to*** angeschlossen werden: *She **said (to me)** that she would be back late.*
Auf ***tell*** muss ein indirektes Objekt (Personenobjekt) folgen. Es wird **ohne *to*** angeschlossen: *She **told me** that she would be back late.*

6 ***Say* oder *tell?* Setze in die Lücke das richtige Verb. Aufgepasst: Es ist nicht immer nur das *present tense* gefragt!**

a) Sue ____________ to her dad that she usually goes to bed early.

b) Andrew ____________ that he had had a wonderful holiday two years ago.

c) What did they ____________ you?

d) Did he ____________ his parents what had happened?

e) Vicky never ______________ her mum anything about school.

f) They didn't ____________ a word to us. Have they ____________ you anything?

7 **Übersetze die folgenden Sätze ins Englische. Schreibe sie in dein Übungsheft.**

a) Jeff sagte mir, dass Sue krank sei.
b) Anne und Michael sagten, dass sie Tennis spielen wollen.
c) Tom sagte mir, dass er keinen Tee mag.
d) Mrs Brown sagt, dass sie jeden Tag früh aufstehe.
e) Julias Eltern sagten ihr, dass sie dieses Kleid nicht in der Schule tragen könne.

Adverbialbestimmungen

Adverbialbestimmungen ändern sich nur, wenn das einleitende Verb in der Vergangenheit steht: *Karen: "It's my birthday* ***today.*** *I'm going to celebrate* ***here.****"* → *Karen told me that it was her birthday* ***that day.*** *She said she was going to celebrate* ***there.***

Es gilt:

here → *there*	*two weeks ago* → *two weeks before*
this/these → *that/those*	*tomorrow* → *the next day*
today → *that day*	*next week* → *the following week*

8 **Formuliere die Sätze in der indirekten Rede.**

Tom said: "I will do my homework tomorrow."

____

Rachel told her friend: "I saw a wonderful dress at my favourite shop today."

____

Paul tells his friend: "I'm going to go to England on holiday this year."

____

Gillian asked: "Have you ever been to the United States?"

____

Meg told her friend: "Yesterday the rain stopped in the evening."

____

Rita said: "I'm going to have my birthday party here."

____

9 ***Listening Comprehension.*** **Höre dir die Sätze auf Track 8 der CD an und wandle sie in die indirekte Rede um. Wann tritt *backshift* ein, wann nicht? Achte auch auf die Veränderung der Orts- und Zeitangaben. Schreibe sie in dein Übungsheft.**

8

10 **Unterstreiche jeweils die richtige Verbform.**

a) *Nikos:* "I haven't seen my Greek relatives for ages." → Nikos said that he wouldn't see/saw/hadn't seen his Greek relatives for ages.

b) *Sue:* "I'm going to play chess all day." → Sue says that she will play/is going to play/is playing chess all day."

c) *Morris:* "I'll be enjoying my work even at age 85." → Morris stated that he would be enjoying/was enjoying/enjoys his work even at age 85.

d) *Peter:* "Where were you last night?" → Peter wanted to know where we have been/had been/were the night before.

e) *Annie:* "I am so bored today!" → Annie complained that she was/had been/am bored yesterday.

f) *Alex:* "I want to travel to India!" → Alex exclaimed that he had been wanting/want/wanted to travel to India.

7.3 Hilfsverben

Modale Hilfsverben in der indirekten Rede

Auch die modalen Hilfsverben ändern sich in der indirekten Rede, wenn das *reporting verb* im *past tense* steht. Die Veränderung folgt dabei festen Regeln: *will* → *would, can* → *could, may* → *might, shall* → *should.*

- *would, could, might, should* und *ought to* bleiben unverändert,
- *must* kann unverändert bleiben (Vorschlag, Annahme oder Schlussfolgerung) oder wird durch *had to* ersetzt (Verpflichtung),
- *needn't* bleibt unverändert oder wird durch *didn't have to* ersetzt,
- *mustn't* bleibt unverändert oder wird durch *wasn't/weren't to* ersetzt.

11 **Wandle die Sätze in die indirekte Rede um.**

Peter: "You should buy that CD."

____

Paul: "It would be nice if I could take you out for dinner, Mary."

____

Father: "You needn't pretend *(so tun als ob)* to be clever."

____

Mother: "You need to take care of Jill while I'm at the dentist's."

____

Brian: "I can come over and babysit."

____

Mum: "It's seven thirty! You mustn't sleep in."

____

12 **Wandle die Sätze in die indirekte Rede um. Verwende immer ein einleitendes Verb im *past tense*. Schreibe in dein Übungsheft.**

Mother: "You mustn't eat so much chocolate."
Bank manager: "You must pay back the money this month."
Peter to Kate: "You must be tired after running the marathon."
Teacher: "You needn't worry about your school report."
Tom: "I'm sure I will enjoy my holidays."
Coach: "I may need some help with the junior team."
The sign said: "You mustn't eat ice cream while riding the tram."
Jane: "I might go to Canada next year."

13 **Wähle die richtige Verbform aus.**

a) "Last night I had to take the dog to the vet."

He told me that he ______________ to take the dog to the vet.

☐ had must ☐ had had ☐ has had

b) "Toby, I might do something to help you."

He said that he ______________ do everything to help his friend.

☐ might ☐ would ☐ could

c) "I can skate and surf."

She told me that she ______________ skate and surf.

☐ could ☐ could have ☐ can

d) "I would go to Rome if I could."

She said that she ______________ go to Rome if she could.

☐ would ☐ should ☐ might

7.4 Fragen und Befehle

Fragen und Befehle wiedergeben

Für Fragen in der indirekten Rede gelten die gleichen Regeln wie für Aussagesätze. Es steht kein Fragezeichen.
Bei **Fragesätzen,** die **mit** einem **Fragewort** (*who, when, where* etc.) eingeleitet werden, steht dasselbe Fragewort auch im indirekten Fragesatz: *Rita: "Lisa, when did you buy this T-shirt?"* → *Rita wanted to know when Lisa had bought that T-shirt.*
Fragen ohne Fragewort werden in der indirekten Rede mit ***if*** oder ***whether*** formuliert: *Tom: "Did you see the latest film with Angelina Jolie, Rob?"* → *Tom asked if/whether Rob had seen the latest film ...*
Aufforderungen und **Befehle** werden mit einem **Infinitiv mit *to*** wiedergegeben: *Teacher: "Be quiet."* → *The teacher told us to be quiet.*
Das gilt auch für Angebote, Einladungen oder Bitten: *Anne: "I'll study hard."* → *Anne promised to study hard.*

14 **Jack stellt Rachel Fragen zu ihrem Ruderwettkampf am vergangenen Wochenende. Formuliere seine Fragen in indirekte Rede um.**

"What kind of sports competition was it?"

Jack asked ______________________________.

"Where did the competition take place?"

____

"Why are there five people in a team?"

____

"Which distance did your race cover?"

____

"Who won the race?"

____

15 **Setze die folgenden Fragen in die indirekte Rede.**

Steve asked you: "Are you good at football?"

Steve asked if/whether I ________________________________.

Stacey wanted to know: "Have you listened to your new CD yet?"

____

Ben: "Ken, do your parents like movies?"

____

Evan: "Bill, have you ever tried to write a weblog?"

____

Bill: "Will you travel to Germany next summer, Andy?"

____

Sara asked me: "Do you like Mexican food?"

____

Evan: "Amy, did you bring enough crisps for the party?"

____

Mum: "Have you practised enough for your concert, John?"

____

Mary: "Jodie, where did you meet your boyfriend for the first time?"

____

Daneesh: "Peter, will you come to Mike's party next weekend?"

____

16 **Setze die folgenden Sätze in die indirekte Rede. Verwende dabei jeweils ein Verb aus dem Wortspeicher.**

to tell – to warn – to advise – to threaten – to promise

Anne: "I'll buy a new book for you."

____

Will: "Don't eat too many chillis. They are very hot *(scharf)*."

____

Father: "I'll take away your computer if you don't pass your exam."

____

Mother: "Lay the table, Ryan."

____

Melanie: "Go and see a doctor."

____

17 **Im Jugendzentrum gelten Regeln, die alle einhalten müssen. Schreibe die Sätze in die indirekte Rede um und verwende als einleitendes Verb *to promise* oder *to be told*. Schreibe in dein Übungsheft.**

Beispiel: ***We promise to/we are told to handle the stereo with care.***

PARTY RULES

Be polite to all guests within these premises.

Don't insult other people.

Don't fight with other party guests.

Help your fellows when necessary.

Don't drink and drive!

8

Der Satz

8.1 Wortstellung

Orts- und Zeitangaben

Ortsangaben stehen immer hinter dem Prädikat am Satzende. Zeitangaben stehen ebenfalls am Satzende, können aber bei Betonung auch am Satzanfang stehen. Stehen beide Angaben, gilt immer: **Ort vor Zeit!**

1 **Schreibe die Sätze in der richtigen Wortstellung auf. Benutze dazu dein Übungsheft.**

a) Mr Smith/teaches/English and history/usually
b) Lily/for breakfast/sometimes/cornflakes/eats
c) English/learn/at school/many children
d) go/we/on Sundays/to the countryside/sometimes
e) interrupt/the children/their teacher/never
f) David and Gordon/at school/on Mondays/usually/play tennis
g) drinks/two cups of coffee/Mrs Taylor/usually/every morning
h) do their homework/the children/always/in the afternoon

2 **Finde den Fehler in der Wortstellung und verbessere den ganzen Satz. Schreibe in dein Übungsheft.**

a) Susie forgets never her homework.
b) Always we go swimming on Saturdays.
c) We eat a lot of ice cream in summer often.
d) Our English teacher forgets never to give us some homework.
e) Tina goes to the supermarket on Tuesdays usually.
f) Anne and Amy visit their mother sometimes together.
g) Always Mr Hope helps his wife in the evening.

3 **Bringe die Satzglieder in die richtige Reihenfolge.**

a) My parents/every day/go to work/at 8 o'clock

____

b) travels/our teacher/to Madrid/in summer/in Spain

____

c) Hanna/her homework/at the desk/does/in her room

____

d) go shopping/I/in the big shopping centre/every Friday/in town

____

e) the school bus/from Monday to Friday/at the bus stop/stops/ at 7:15 a.m.

____

f) in summer/often/the children/at a big sports centre/go swimming/in town

____

8.2 Satzverknüpfungen

Beiordnende und unterordnende Konjunktionen

Ein breiter Vorrat an Satzverknüpfungen *(link words/connectives)* erweitert das Ausdrucksvermögen und bietet mehr Möglichkeiten, eine Idee zu formulieren.

4 **Wähle aus dem Wortspeicher die richtige Satzverknüpfung und setze sie in die Lücken ein.**

although – as if – neither ... nor – whereas – provided that – when – supposing that – after – as soon as – until – but – moreover

a) The alarm was raised ____________ the fire was discovered.

b) You can have a passenger on a motorcycle ____________________ the passenger wears a helmet.

c) I like him, ____________ he doesn't like me.

d) ____________ I had locked up, I went straight to bed.

e) My sister was ill. She ____________ ate ____________ drank ____________ she was well again.

f) We had a great holiday _______________ the weather was bad.

g) ____________________ I lent you my car, would that of any help?

h) Our old house was sunny and bright ______________ the new one is dark and gloomy.

i) ____________ I saw his face, I knew I'd met him before.

j) I don't understand why she doesn't talk to me anymore. __________ ________, she acts ____________ she didn't know me at all.

5 **Unterstreiche die richtige Konjunktion in den folgenden Sätzen.**

a) We can have lunch as if/since/as soon as we've finished this.

b) I enjoyed the film either/although/whereas it was very sad.

c) I didn't phone you because/as though/or it was too late.

d) Pat got ready thus/while/before I was preparing dinner.

e) Just do even if/as/and I told you.

f) Unless/When/If there's a problem, I won't disturb you.

6 **Formuliere die Sätze mithilfe der Konjunktionen in Klammern um. Schreibe in dein Übungsheft.**

a) I didn't call you. I'd lost your phone number. (since)
b) Last week there was a violent storm. It caused widespread flooding. (because)
c) First I went to Boston. Then I flew to Houston. (after)
d) Perhaps we will miss the last train. In that case we will take a taxi. (supposing)
e) The Johnsons had an alarm system installed. Nobody would break into the house again. (so that)

7 **Übersetze die folgenden Sätze mit der richtigen Konjunktion ins Englische. Schreibe die Sätze in dein Übungsheft.**

a) Ich habe dieses Buch gekauft, um (= damit ich ...) mein Englisch zu verbessern.
b) Die Kinder benahmen sich, als ob nichts passiert wäre.
c) Sarah war vorsichtig, während Christopher viele Fehler machte.
d) Ich wusste, dass sie wütend war, sobald ich ihr Gesicht sah.
e) Sofern das Wetter nicht besser wird, werden wir nicht ins Freie gehen können.

8.3 Bedingungssätze

Typen von *if*-Sätzen

Es gibt drei Arten von Bedingungssätzen *(conditional clauses):*

- **Typ I:** erfüllbar; es steht im *if*-Satz *past tense,* im Hauptsatz *will-future,*
- **Typ II:** nicht erfüllbar; *if*-Satz: *simple present,* Hauptsatz: *conditional I,*
- **Typ III:** nicht mehr erfüllbar; *if*-Satz: *past perfect,* Hauptsatz: *conditional perfect.*

8 **Bilde vollständige Bedingungssätze vom Typ I. Verbinde die *if*-Satzteile mit den Hauptsatzteilen. Schreibe die Sätze in dein Übungsheft.**

***if*-Satz**	**Hauptsatz**
I (tell) you the truth	she (be) angry
you (not/call) her	we (get) good marks
Susan (stay) longer	you (be) shocked
we (work) hard	he (not/pass) the exams
he (not/do) his homework	she (miss) the bus

9 **Fülle die Lücken mit den richtigen Zeitformen und *when* oder *if*.**

a) I ______________ (be) there ________ (Bedingung) you ______________ (arrive) at 7 o'clock.

b) Sally ______________ (read) the book ________ (Zeitpunkt) she ______________ (get) it.

c) ________ (Zeitpunkt) she ______________ (arrive) at the hotel, she ______________ (meet) him.

d) ________ (Bedingung) you ______________ (make) too many mistakes, you ________________ (not/pass) the exam.

10 **Vervollständige die folgenden Sätze mit einem Bedingungssatz Typ II. Aus verneinten Aussagen werden bejahte *if*-Sätze und umgekehrt.**

a) It rains. If it ________________, we could go by bike.

b) I have a lot to do today. If I ________________ so much to do, we could go out.

c) I don't understand these questions. If I ________________ them, I could help you with your homework.

d) The world isn't a better place. If the world ________________ a better place, there would be no wars.

11 **Übersetze die folgenden Sätze ins Englische und achte auf die richtige Übersetzung von *würde*. Schreibe in dein Übungsheft.**

a) Wenn ich mehr lesen würde, wäre ich besser informiert.
b) Wenn Sally Pete Geld leihen würde, würde er es ihr nicht zurückgeben.
c) Was würdest du deinem Brieffreund schreiben, wenn du von ihm einen Brief bekommen würdest?
d) Wir könnten zusammen essen, wenn wir uns treffen würden.

12 **Wähle die richtige Form und streiche die falsche durch.**

a) If you would live/lived in England, you would have school every afternoon.

b) Can you phone me if you get/will get to the hotel?

c) John could be happier if he would be/was back at home.

d) If you wait/would wait a minute, I will go with you.

e) If you went by train, it would be/will be quicker than by bus.

13 **Kreuze an, um welchen Typ von Bedingungssatz es sich handelt.**

	Typ I	Typ II	Typ III
a) If I moved to London, I would speak English all day.	☐	☐	☐
b) If you turn the handle, the door opens.	☐	☐	☐
c) If you buy that huge wardrobe, you will need a bigger room.	☐	☐	☐
d) If you loved chocolate, you would enjoy that cake.	☐	☐	☐
e) If I had saved some money, I would have flown to Australia.	☐	☐	☐

14 **Setze die Verben in Klammern in die richtige Zeit.**

a) If it rains, I ____________________ (take) my umbrella.

b) I ________________________ (close) all schools if I were Prime Minister.

c) Would you be glad if I ___________________ (buy) your old car?

d) If you don't have a book to read, I ___________________ (lend) you one.

e) If he had played a bad concert, his mother _________________________ ____________________ (be disappointed).

f) _________________________ (you / read) more if you had more time?

g) I couldn't have come today if my father _______________________ (not/ lend) me his car.

h) My friends would have laughed at me if they ________________ (see) me trying to ride a unicycle *(Einrad)*.

i) Your hair _______________________ (look) better if you hadn't cut it.

15 **Bilde Bedingungssätze und schreibe sie in dein Übungsheft.**

a) to get married/one day/you – to play the violin/I (Typ I)
b) Sal/to read/the book – not/to go/to see the movie/he (Typ III)
c) to meet/Brad Pitt/you – to ask/you/for an autograph (Typ II, question!)
d) to break her leg/my mother/not – she/to travel/to Italy (Typ III)
e) you/to read/that travel guide – you/to know/a little more about California (Typ II)

16 **Vervollständige die Bedingungssätze mit den angegebenen Wendungen. Schreibe die Sätze in dein Übungsheft.**

get fat – take it back – not meet her again – go and see a doctor – find a spider in my bed

If you are ill, you ...
I would panic if I ...
If I were you, I ...
If you eat too much, you ...
If you shouldn't like the DVD, I ...

17 **Wandle die folgenden Aussagen in Bedingungssätze um. Wähle den richtigen Typ und schreibe die Sätze in dein Übungsheft.**
Beispiel: ***I was so tired, I didn't stay up to watch that movie.*** → ***If I hadn't been so tired, I would have stayed up to watch that movie.***

a) My brother is not going to buy this computer – it's too expensive.
b) Please stay at home tonight so that we can watch that film together.
c) Sorry I didn't go to the restaurant with you. I didn't feel well that day.
d) The Millers missed their flight because there was so much traffic on the way to the airport.

8.4 Relativsätze

Who, that, which* und *whose

Relativsätze werden durch ein Relativpronomen eingeleitet: ***Who*** wird für **Personen** verwendet, ***which*** steht bei **Dingen.** Sowohl *who* als auch *which* können durch ***that*** ersetzt werden: *This is the girl who/that lost her exercise book. We have a car which/that is big enough to seat seven people.* ***Whose*** drückt eine Zugehörigkeit oder einen Besitz aus: *That's the girl **whose** sister won the song contest last year.*
Relativsätze, die man nicht weglassen kann, ohne dass der Satz seinen Sinn verliert, heißen **notwendige Relativsätze** *(defining relative clauses).* Es steht kein Komma; das Relativpronomen muss stehen: *He was the man who saved my life.*
Stehen im Relativsatz Informationen, die weggelassen werden können, ohne dass sich dadurch die Aussage des Hauptsatzes ändert, handelt es sich um **nicht notwendige Relativsätze** *(non-defining relative clauses).* Das Komma muss stehen: *The book, which I am reading at the moment, is very interesting.*
Ist das Relativpronomen das Objekt eines notwendigen Relativsatzes, kann es weggelassen werden. Solche Relativsätze nennt man ***contact clauses:*** *The trip [that] we took to San Francisco was very interesting.*

18 **Setze das fehlende Relativpronomen ein.**

a) Frederic is a boy __________ can sing and play the guitar.

b) Jason's mother is a nurse __________ works at the hospital.

c) They showed a film __________ was brilliant.

d) This is Margret __________ aunt works in the bakery.

e) This is my friend Ron __________ bought a blue bike.

f) Mr Harold is the neighbour ____________ dogs are always barking.

g) Mrs Richard is the teacher __________ went to Rome last year.

19 **Setze das fehlende Relativpronomen ein. Entscheide, ob es sich um einen notwendigen (nR) oder einen nicht notwendigen Relativsatz (nnR) handelt.**

	nR	nnR
Do you see the bike __________ is in front of the shop?	☐	☐
This is the boy __________ helps me with my homework.	☐	☐
The homework, __________ we got last week, is difficult.	☐	☐
Elvis Presley, __________ was a famous pop star, died in 1977.	☐	☐
Have you got a knife __________ is sharp enough for the bread?	☐	☐
They stole my wallet __________ was in my jacket.	☐	☐
Margaret Thatcher, __________ was called the "Iron Lady", was British prime minister from 1979 until 1990.	☐	☐

20 **Mache aus den zwei Sätzen einen Satz, indem du sie mit einem Relativpronomen verbindest. Welche Sätze sind *contact clauses?* Kennzeichne sie durch Einklammern des Relativpronomens. Schreibe in dein Übungsheft.**

a) A woman was opening the door. She was wearing red jeans.
b) A policeman stopped my bike. He was very nice.
c) Sue is wearing an anorak. I like it.
d) Some pupils took their exams. They weren't difficult at all.
e) You bought some apples. How much were they?
f) You gave me a CD. I can't find it anywhere.
g) You made this cake. It was wonderful.
h) I have got a friend. He is very good at repairing computers.

21 **Verbessere die Sätze, indem du das falsche Relativpronomen durchstreichst und den Satz richtig in deinem Übungsheft aufschreibst.**

Beispiel: ***That's the school ~~to~~ that I go. → That's the school that I go to.***

a) Is that the girl who's photo was in the papers yesterday?
b) That's the hotel at whose we stayed.
c) Where is the lady which lost her purse?
d) Where is the pen with that I always write?
e) That's the boy who sister is good at French.

22 **Übersetze die deutschen Relativsätze ins Englische.**

a) Is that the family deren Sohn gestern im Fernsehen war?

---

b) Where is the computer magazine das ich gerade gekauft habe?

---

c) That's the girl neben dem ich in der Schule sitze.

---

d) The house das meine Eltern gekauft haben has a garden.

---

23 **Übersetze und schreibe in dein Übungsheft.**

a) Das Haus, das blaue Türen hat, ist sehr groß.
b) Autofahrer, die viel Alkohol trinken, können sehr gefährlich sein.
c) Ich habe das Mädchen, dessen Schwester Mary heißt, gestern in der Bücherei getroffen.
d) Jenny kochte ein Gericht, das sie in Italien probiert hatte.
e) Der Junge, der sehr gut Fußball spielen kann, brach sich das Bein.
f) Sie las ein Buch, das ihre Freunde ihr empfohlen hatten.

24 **Füge die richtigen Relativpronomen ein und setze Kommas, wo sie notwendig sind. Achtung: Ein Satz kommt ganz ohne Relativpronomen aus.**

a) Our school ________ is located across a wonderful park ________ is old but beautiful.

b) It was my sister ________ gave me tickets for the rock concert.

c) The people ________ I work with ________ are very nice.

d) Last week I took my little niece to the cinema ________ is just around the corner from where I live.

25 **Setze im folgenden Text Kommas, wo sie notwendig sind.**

a) The woman who lives next door writes cookery books.

b) Where is the box that I bought in India?

c) Mrs Bell who surprised us all is a most lovely woman.

d) The teacher spoke to the pupils whose work was quite bad.

e) The Channel Islands which consist of four main islands lie in the English Channel.

26 **Beende die folgenden Sätze mit einem selbst ausgedachten Relativsatz. Schreibe sie in dein Übungsheft.**

I'll always remember the day ...
I met somebody ...
I got the job ...
I don't agree with the opinion ...
I don't like people ...

8.5 Sätze mit Gerundium, Partizip und Infinitiv

Satzverkürzungen

Das **Gerundium** wird durch Anhängen von *-ing* an das Verb gebildet. Im Satz wird es ähnlich wie ein Substantiv verwendet: Es kann Subjekt oder Objekt sein. Zahlreiche Verben, Substantive und Ausdrücke haben das Gerundium nach sich: *Can you imagine **travelling** in space? She has a lot of experience in **driving** a truck.*
Das **Partizip Präsens** *(present participle,* ebenfalls *-ing*-Form) und das **Partizip Perfekt** *(past participle)* können einen Relativsatz ersetzen: *The girl **performing** (= who performs) on stage is my sister. Photos **taken** on Mars (= that were taken on Mars) were transmitted to the earth.*
Auch mithilfe einer **Infinitivkonstruktion** (mit oder ohne *to*) kann im Englischen ein Sachverhalt verkürzt ausgedrückt werden (insbesondere bei Verben des Denkens, Wünschens, Aufforderns, Veranlassens und Verursachens): *Father allowed me **to go** to the party. We heard them **argue** over money.*

27 **Verbinde die Sätze mithilfe des Gerundiums. Schreibe in dein Übungsheft.**
Beispiel: ***My sister stays out late every Saturday night. She enjoys it. → My sister enjoys staying out late every Saturday night.***

a) Sally might become a movie star one day. Her boyfriend doesn't even like the idea of it.
b) My sister never saves any money. She isn't good at it.
c) Laura wants to move out when she's 18. She's talking of it already.
d) Rick spends a lot of money on books. His mum is very fond of it.
e) Samuel has to go to the dentist's again. He is frightened about it.
f) The girls want to go out for dinner. They suggest it.
g) Linda reads bedtime stories to her nephew and niece. They like it.

28 **Übersetze und verwende das Gerundium. Schreibe in dein Übungsheft.**

a) Wie wär's, wenn wir heute Nachmittag Eis essen gehen?
b) Ich habe keine Schwierigkeiten, Englisch zu lernen.
c) Interessierst du dich dafür, Fußball zu spielen?
d) Denkst du darüber nach, dir einen neuen Computer zu kaufen?
e) Manche Mädchen träumen davon, Pilotin zu werden.
f) Sie hat eine Menge Erfahrung im Unterrichten.

29 **Gerundium oder Infinitiv? Ergänze die richtige Verbform!**

a) I can't stand ______________ (clean) the bathroom.

b) I prefer ___________ (go) for a walk to _________ (watch) TV.

c) It is right ______________ (help) the poor.

d) It's not worth ______________ (buy) lottery tickets.

e) I was delighted ______________ (hear) that I had won the lottery.

30 **Verkürze die Sätze mithilfe einer Partizipialkonstruktion.**

a) The boy who plays football is dreaming of a big career.

____

b) The pool that was built in our backyard wasn't worth its money.

____

c) Laura knows the boy who lives next door very well.

____

d) Because I was reading a good book, I didn't answer the phone.

____

31 **Höre dir Track 9 auf der CD an und setze die zum Gerundium gehörende passende Präposition ein.**

9

a) She has a lot of experience __________ dancing.

b) Betty has a good method __________ learning.

c) Father has a reason __________ asking me twice about my results in the last maths exam.

d) They have a chance __________ winning the championship.

e) Instead __________ watching TV you'd better go jogging.

f) Wash your hands __________ eating.

g) There's no reason __________ complaining all the time.

32 **Richtig oder falsch? Kreuze an, ob die Sätze richtig oder falsch sind. Verbessere die Fehler und schreibe die Sätze richtig in dein Übungsheft.**

	right	wrong
a) How about to travel to Hawaii next summer?	☐	☐
b) I don't have an interest in study, I only want to play computer games.	☐	☐
c) There must be a reason for cooking potatoes.	☐	☐
d) Ian spent a lot of time to try to find a present.	☐	☐
e) He hates living in the countryside.	☐	☐
f) He hates to live in the city.	☐	☐
g) She left the house without to eat breakfast.	☐	☐
h) It's no use to complain about bad teachers.	☐	☐

33 **Infinitiv oder Gerundium? Setze ein.**

a) It's not worth ________________ (buy) that book. It's boring.

b) My mother forced me ________________ (study) some English vocabulary.

c) Dad permitted Hannah ________________ (go) to the party.

d) Would you mind ________________ (help) me with the dishes?

e) I can hardly resist ________________ (eat) another ice cream.

f) Instead of ________________ (watch) TV, you should better go swimming!

g) Children usually love ________________ (play) games.

h) Cara was the best pupil ________________ (play) the violin.

34 **Verkürze die Sätze mithilfe einer Partizipialkonstruktion. Schreibe in dein Übungsheft.**

a) When I arrived at my friends' house, I was welcomed by their dog.
b) As he noticed that the old lady felt sick, Jim called an ambulance.
c) Jim, who hasn't worked in the garden for a while, felt tired after mowing the lawn.
d) Toby, who had eaten too much chocolate, felt awful.

35 Bedeutungsunterschiede bei der Verwendung von Gerundium oder Infinitiv. Welche Übersetzung ist richtig?

a) Mein Freund hat aufgehört zu rauchen.

☐ My boyfriend stopped smoking.

☐ My boyfriend stopped to smoke.

b) Früher ist er immer zeitig aufgestanden.

☐ He used to get up early.

☐ He is used to getting up early.

c) Wir versuchten, die Schlüssel zu finden.

☐ We tried to find the keys.

☐ We tried finding the keys.

d) Letzten Winter habe ich Snowboarden ausprobiert.

☐ I tried to snowboard last winter.

☐ I tried snowboarding last winter.

e) Ich muss daran denken, Tee einzukaufen.

☐ I must remember to buy some tea.

☐ I must remember buying some tea.

f) Du hast vergessen, dass du Jill getroffen hast, oder?

☐ You forgot meeting Jill, didn't you?

☐ You forgot to meet Jill, didn't you?

g) Der Premierminister redete unaufhörlich über seine Außenpolitik.

☐ The Prime Minister went on to talk about his foreign policy.

☐ The Prime Minister went on talking about his foreign policy.

36 **Finde die Fehler in den Sätzen und verbessere sie. Schreibe die richtigen Sätze in dein Übungsheft. Tipp: Ein Satz ist richtig!**

a) Instead to go out, you should concentrate on your exams.
b) Being sunny, Andy decided to go cycling.
c) Feeling hungry, the teenagers stopped for a hamburger.
d) It's no use to try it again.
e) Seeing how dark it was, Timmy felt nervous.
f) Being long and boring, the students didn't want to read the novel.

37 **Schreibe den farbig markierten Satzteil mithilfe einer Partizipialkonstruktion in deinem Übungsheft um.**

a) The dress which is worn by Cecil must have cost a fortune.
b) Tom is confused by modern technology and doesn't want to buy a computer.
c) The text is written in Chinese and is quite hard to understand.
d) We did not know which road to take and had to ask a resident.
e) Jane couldn't sleep, so she got up and walked around.
f) After he had completed his work, Mr Taylor went for a walk.

38 **Verändere den markierten Satzteil, indem du das Gerundium und die angegebenen Wörter verwendest. Schreibe die Sätze vollständig in dein Übungsheft.**

on – by – in spite of – apart from

a) My parents believe that I get excellent marks if I learn more.
b) Victoria was working hard for her finals, but she failed them with flying colours.
c) When Jill saw her sister after all these years, she started to cry.
d) She is not only a talented musician but also a gifted photographer.

8.6 Sätze mit dem Verb „lassen“

make und _let_

Der Ausdruck *to make sb. do sth.* bedeutet „jemanden dazu bringen, etwas zu tun“. *To let sb. do sth.* heißt „jemandem erlauben, etwas zu tun“. Die Konstruktion *to have/get sth. done* verwendest du, wenn man etwas nicht selbst macht, sondern von jemand anderem machen lässt.

39 ***Make* oder *let*? Setze das richtige Verb in die Lücke.**

a) Let's watch a funny film on DVD. I'm sure it will __________ you laugh, and laughing __________ you feel better.

b) __________ me know whether you would like to join us for a party at the beach: Dad __________ me have his car tonight.

c) You cannot be __________ to drink alcoholic beverages if you don't really want it. Don't __________ your friends persuade you!

d) Don't be too late tonight again! If you __________ this happen too often, we'll __________ you come home earlier next time – or even worse – we won't __________ you go out at all.

e) Don't __________ yourself be fooled by Jake. He may definitely _______ you feel unhappy if only you __________ him.

40 **Übersetze die folgenden Sätze im Übungsheft ins Englische.**

a) Ein schrecklicher Lärm ließ mich letzte Nacht nicht schlafen.
b) Ich lasse meine Haare jeden Monat schneiden.
c) Warum lässt du dein Motorrad nicht reparieren?
d) Meine Eltern ließen mich letzte Woche im Garten arbeiten.
e) Ihre Mutter wollte Sue zuerst nicht gehen lassen.

8.7 Inversion

Wortumstellung zur Betonung

Einige negative oder einschränkende adverbiale Bestimmungen können auch am Satzanfang stehen, um eine besondere Betonung zu erzielen: Erst steht die adverbiale Bestimmung, dann Hilfsverb und Subjekt: *I have never had such a shock* → *Never have I had such a shock*. Ist kein Hilfsverb vorhanden, verwendest du eine Form von *do: She hardly goes out these days* → *Hardly does she go out these days.*

41 **Schreibe die nachfolgenden Sätze um, indem du den Satz mit dem farbig markierten Adverb einleitest. Schreibe in dein Übungsheft.**

a) Robert rarely stayed at home to do school work.
b) He never thought about what his future might bring.
c) He had hardly gone to university when he had to work harder.
d) He has seldom felt so determined to be successful.

42 **Schreibe die folgenden Sätze in deinem Übungsheft um, indem du die Inversion verwendest.**

a) He had never believed any stories about this fascinating city. → Never had he ...
b) He hadn't seen any skyscrapers either because he came from a small town.
c) He could hardly believe his eyes when he saw the Empire State Building.
d) If you had told me about your problems, I could have helped you.
e) If you should happen to be around, come and see us.

43 **Vervollständige die Sätze mit dem passenden Ausdruck.**

the power of the punch – the force of the wind – his story/to sound strange – the famine/to be serious

a) Such ______________________________ that dozens of roofs were lifted off.

b) So ______________________________ that the United Nations sent food and water supplies to that area.

c) Such ______________________________ that his opponent was knocked out.

d) So ______________________________ that no one could possibly believe him.

44 **Formuliere diese Sätze mit Inversion so um, dass sie wegfällt.**

a) Never would my parents treat me so badly.

____

b) Seldom had he seen such a sunset.

____

c) Should this not work, ask somebody to help you.

____

d) Not only did Jane want to go out with Burke, but she even phoned him twice a day.

____

____

9

Wortschatz

9.1 Präpositionen

Zeit, Ort und Richtung

Präpositionen der Zeit *(prepositions of time)* geben an, wann etwas geschieht, Präpositionen des Ortes *(prepositions of place)* geben an, wo etwas geschieht oder wo sich etwas befindet. Präpositionen der Richtung *(prepositions of direction)* drücken eine Bewegung aus.

1 **Welches sind die richtigen Präpositionen? Setze ein.**

um drei Uhr	↔	_________ three o'clock
am Montag	↔	_________ Monday
morgens	↔	_________ the morning
nachts	↔	_________ night
im Sommer	↔	_________ summer
an Ostern	↔	_________ Easter
während des Mittagessens	↔	_________ lunch
mittwochs	↔	_________ Wednesdays
am 15. Oktober	↔	_________ 15th October
nach dem Frühstück	↔	_________ breakfast
an Weihnachten	↔	_________ Christmas

2 **Bilde vollständige Sätze und ergänze dabei die Präposition. Stelle die Ort- und Zeitangaben ans Ende des Satzes. Schreibe in dein Übungsheft.**

a) have – a big brunch – ________ the weekend – we

b) in the garden – my friend and I – ________ the afternoon – play hockey

c) to school – ________ the morning – I – walk – every day

d) my friends – ________ December – I – in London – love to visit

e) and I – ________ winter – my parents – to Italy – go

3 **Füge die fehlenden Präpositionen des Ortes in den Dialog ein.**

Sue: "Mum, I can't find my mobile phone. I have looked everywhere ________ my room and it's not ________ the kitchen, either. It's not ________ the shelves and not ____________ the coffee maker. I even looked __________ the fridge." *(in/in/auf/vor/hinter)*

Mum: "I think I saw it somewhere ________ the living-room, __________ the television or on the table ____________ the TV guide and my new book." *(in/neben/zwischen)*

Sue: "Ah, there it is! I left it ____________ the mirror in the hall! Thanks, mum!" *(gegenüber)*

4 **Lies die deutschen Wendungen, dann suche die passenden Orts- und Zeitangaben auf Englisch. Verbinde die richtigen englischen Übersetzungen und die deutschen Angaben mit Linien und trage die fehlende Präposition ein.**

um drei Uhr	__________ Tuesday
rund um das Haus	__________ the window
am Dienstag	__________ spring
im März	__________ the house
gegen das Fenster	__________ the station
im Frühling	__________ the morning
zwischen ein und zwei Uhr	__________ March
am Morgen	__________ breakfast
vor dem Abendessen	__________ the weekend
am Bahnhof vorbei	__________ three o'clock
während des Frühstücks	get __________ the car
über die Brücke	__________ 2011
am Wochenende	__________ one and two o'clock
2011	__________ dinner
aus dem Auto steigen	__________ the bridge

9.2 *False friends*

Ähnliche Wörter im Deutschen und Englischen

Einige Wörter im Englischen sind deutschen Wörtern sehr ähnlich, haben jedoch eine ganz andere Bedeutung. Diese sogenannten falschen Freunde *(false friends)* musst du auswendig lernen.

5 **Schlage die englischen Wörter in deinem Wörterbuch nach und suche die richtige Übersetzung für das falsche, aber ähnliche deutsche Wort.**

ordinary → ______________

ordinär → ______________

rent → ______________

Rente → ______________

to wonder → ______________

sich wundern → ______________

personal → ______________

Personal → ______________

receipt → ______________

Rezept → ______________

chips → ______________

Chips → ______________

6 **Setze das richtige englische Wort in die Lücken.**

a) How much is the *(Miete)* ______________ for this flat?

b) Your *(Kritik)* ______________ of his work is not justified.

c) What's your *(Meinung)* ______________ of the new film?

d) What's the *(Bedeutung)* ______________ of that sign over there? – It says your're not allowed to use your *(Handy)* ______________.

e) Sara has worked very hard this term and indeed, her *(Noten)* ______________ have improved a lot.

7 **Welches ist das richtige Wort? Kreuze an.**

a) If a doctor thinks that some medicine might help, he writes a

☐ receipt ☐ prescription ☐ note

b) The workers of a company are called

☐ pension ☐ personal ☐ staff

c) The money somebody receives after retiring is called

☐ rent ☐ brand ☐ pension

d) If you are asking for a new job, the person who finally decides is called

☐ chief ☐ boss ☐ chef

8 **In jedem Satz steckt ein Fehler. Unterstreiche ihn und ersetze den falschen Begriff durch den richtigen. Erstelle dann in deinem Übungsheft eine Liste mit den falsch verwendeten Begriffen und übersetze diese.**

a) What's the actual score? – It's 2:3 for our team. → ______________

b) The murder could escape easily. → ______________

c) At the moment, I'm reading Harry Potter books. It's a very interesting lecture. → ______________

d) The department store's personal is taking a trip to the castle tomorrow. → ______________

e) Kate wondered when Kevin told her about his problems. He had never done that before. → ______________

9.3 *British vs. American English*

Unterschiedliche Wörter in USA und GB

Für die gleiche Sache werden in Großbritannien und den USA oft unterschiedliche Wörter verwendet. Auch bei der Schreibweise gibt es teils wichtige Unterschiede.

9 **Ergänze die Tabelle.**

BE	AE	deutsche Bedeutung
	chips	
biscuit	cookie	
		Film
	notebook	
Lift		
	fall	
	subway	
		Lastwagen
	trash	
holiday		
petrol		

10 **Die folgenden Wörter stehen in der britischen Schreibweise. Wie werden sie im amerikanischen Englisch geschrieben? Schreibe in dein Heft.**

colour – theatre – monologue – traveling – programme – flavour – catalogue – colonialise

9.4 *Useful phrases*

Wörter und Wendungen zur Textanalyse

Wenn du einen Text analysieren musst, können dir bestimmte Wörter und Wendungen weiterhelfen, dich in Diskussionen und beim Schreiben von Texten sicher und abwechslungsreich auszudrücken.

11 **Mit den folgenden Sätzen kann man jemandem zustimmen, widersprechen oder seine Meinung erfragen. Entwerfe in deinem Übungsheft eine Tabelle wie angegeben und führe sie weiter, indem du die Sätze richtig einträgst.**

That's quite right. – How do you feel/think about this? – I don't think that's right. – I may be wrong but ... – That's my view exactly. – I can't agree with you more. – What is your view on the matter? – I agree (entirely). – Do you agree with that? – I don't agree at all. – That's not the way I see it. – Would you like to add anything?

Zustimmung äußern	Ablehnung äußern	Meinung erfragen
	I don't agree at all.	

12 **Nimm zu den folgenden Aussagen Stellung, indem du mithilfe der genannten Ausdrücke deine Meinung äußerst. Schreibe in dein Übungsheft.**

I (don't) think that – I believe that – I find it strange that – I'm sure that – in my opinion – I suppose that

a) Teenagers should have their own TV sets.
b) Pubs should be stricter when it comes to under-age drinking.
c) Drugs should be legalized.
d) Children should be disciplined if they misbehave.
e) It should be strictly forbidden to use your cell phone at school.

13 **Verbinde die Satzhälften sinnvoll miteinander und schreibe die vollständigen Sätze in dein Übungsheft.**

You have to look at the pros and cons	like clones, so to speak.
I'm against	in other words, everyone can afford it these days.
I'm sure	of legalizing drugs.
On the one hand, using guns should be legalized,	I would like to thank everyone present.
Cosmetic surgery is no longer for the rich and famous,	that something could be done about animal experiments.
In conclusion,	on the other hand, gun control is also necessary.
They looked all very similar,	they agreed with us.

14 **Lies den Text und bringe die Sätze in die richtige Reihenfolge, indem du die einzelnen Aussagen sinnvoll anordnest. Wähle dazu die passenden Ausdrücke aus dem Wortspeicher und schreibe in dein Übungsheft.**

in conclusion – first – finally/at last – in summary – next

Jessica was excluded from school for a few days. She wasn't allowed to attend normal lessons. She was sent to the headmaster, who told her that she had failed to bring credit upon herself, the other pupils and the school by her appearance. Jessica appeared at school with pink hair, black clothes and rings on several parts of her body. The code of conduct states that pupils must wear a school uniform and shouldn't expose themselves.

9.5 Wortfelder und Wortfamilien

Gruppen von Wörtern

Ein **Wortfeld** bezeichnet eine Gruppe von Wörtern, die inhaltlich sinnverwandt sind. Sie werden aus einem Oberbegriff *(group term)* und den dazu passenden Unterbegriffen gebildet.
Eine Gruppe von Wörtern, die sich aus der gleichen Wurzel entwickelt haben, bezeichnet man als **Wortfamilie.** Durch Vorsilben *(prefixes)* oder Nachsilben *(suffixes)* entstehen aus einem Wortstamm neue Wörter.

15 **Finde den passenden Oberbegriff für die Wortgruppe.**

a) castle – lighthouse – pyramid – monastery → ______________

b) carrot – tomato – cucumber – lettuce → ______________

c) basketball – rugby – gymnastics – high jump → ______________

d) drill – screwdriver – hammer – handsaw → ______________

e) ball – doll – stuffed animal – marbles → ______________

16 **Wortbildung. Kreuze die richtige Lösung an.**

a) Welche Wortbildung drückt das Gegenteil von *fortunate* aus?

☐ infortunate ☐ disfortunate ☐ unfortunate ☐ imfortunate

b) Wie heißt das zu *terror* gehörige Adjektiv?

☐ terrorist ☐ terrible ☐ terrorize ☐ terrify

c) Wie heißt das Substantiv zu *true*?

☐ truly ☐ truism ☐ truth ☐ trust

d) Welche Wortbildung für das Gegenteil von *active* ist zulässig?

☐ disactive ☐ irractive ☐ inactive ☐ unactive

e) Welches dieser Wörter bildet KEINE Ableitung auf *-able?*

☐ fashion ☐ health ☐ respect ☐ count

f) Welches der folgenden Adjektive gibt es nicht?

☐ playful ☐ helpful ☐ tactful ☐ youngful

g) Welche negative Wortbildung ist richtig?

☐ unpossible ☐ dispossible ☐ impossible ☐ inpossible

h) Welche zwei (!) Adjektive sind falsch gebildet?

☐ unbelievable ☐ uncountable ☐ unpolite ☐ unmobile

17 **Lies dir den folgenden kurzen Text durch. Finde für die farbig markierten Wörter in deinem einsprachigen Wörterbuch ein Synonym. Schreibe sie in dein Übungsheft.**

Slowly, the drink began to take over, and things got worse for Steve. His behaviour was becoming appalling. One night at a local pub, a fight broke out, and he was, of course, involved in it. Only a few minutes later he was outside being questioned by the police. Then he had to spend several hours at the police station. He was finally released. The next day, however, he was at the pub again, having a ravenous appetite for a drink – a beer that was. Then it dawned on Steve. What kind of person was he, being at a pub every day and his parents not knowing about it. He might end up a lonely and desperate alcoholic.

9.6 Arbeit mit dem Wörterbuch

Ein- und zweisprachige Wörterbücher

Je schwieriger die englischen Texte werden, die im Unterricht drankommen, desto wichtiger ist es, mit einem Wörterbuch umgehen zu können.

18 **Leitwörter im Wörterbuch: Links oben auf der Seite steht das erste Wort der Seite, rechts oben das letzte Wort der Seite. Ein Wort passt jeweils nicht zwischen die folgenden Leitwörter. Streiche es durch.**

a) disgrace – disposal: disorder – disgust – dish – disk – discuss
b) familiar – farm: farewell – fan club – family – false – far
c) horse – house: hot – horror – host – hour – hostility
d) keyboard – king: kill – kick – key – kind – kilo
e) life – light: lift – light – lie – lightning
f) ocean – off: odd – occur – odour – ocelot – of

19 **Lies diesen Wörterbucheintrag durch. Welchen Bestandteil des Eintrags bezeichnen die farbigen Großbuchstaben? Schreibe in dein Übungsheft.**

crack [kræk] (← A) *n* (← B) **1** ~ (in sth.) a line on the surface of sth. where it has broken but not split into separate parts (← C): *This plate has a crack in it. Cracks began to appear in the walls.* (← D) **2** a narrow space or opening: *The door opened a crack.* **3** a sudden loud noise: *the sharp crack of a shot* **4** ~ (at sth.) ~ (at doing sth.) *informal* (← E) an occasion when you try to do sth.: *He hopes to have another crack at the world record this year.* **5** ~ (on sth.) a sharp blow than can be heard: *She fell over and got a nasty crack on the head.* **6** [U] (← F) a powerful, illegal drug; *syn* cocaine (← G): *a crack addict* **7** *informal* a joke, especially a critical one: *He made a very unfair crack about her looks. idm* **at the crack of dawn** (← H) *informal* very early in the morning
cracked (← I) [krækt] *adj* **1** damaged with lines but not yet broken: *a cracked cup* **2** [not before *n*] *(informal)* crazy: *He must be cracked.*

Umgang mit Texten

10.1 Texte verstehen

Keywords und W-Fragen

Sowohl beim Hören *(listening comprehension)* als auch beim Lesen gilt: Sei gründlich und konzentriert. Lies einen Text immer mehrmals durch und achte beim Lesen/Hören auf sogenannte **Schlüsselbegriffe** *(keywords)*, also Wörter, die den Hauptgedanken bzw. das Thema eines Texts bezeichnen.
Die fünf wichtigsten Fragen an einen Text, die sogenannten **W-Fragen,** helfen dir dabei. Sie lauten: *Who? What? When? Where? Why?*
Who reports about what?
Who is involved?
What is the text about?
When does/did the event happen?
Where does the story take place?
Why does something happen? And/or why is it important to report on?

1 **Lies diesen Text durch.**

At the beginning of the last century, moving pictures were invented. At first, these pictures were recorded without sound. In a modern movie, however, sound effects and music are as important as the story itself. Modern movies also use a lot of special effects to attract publicity. And, of course, actors and actresses are very important. Famous movie stars earn a lot of money and often live in a world of their own.

2 **Welche der folgenden Überschriften passt zu dem Text in Übung 1?**

☐ An unreal world

☐ Stars in the universe

☐ A short history of movies

3 **Hier ist die Reihenfolge durcheinandergeraten. Sortiere die Sätze so, dass der Text einen Sinn ergibt. Schreibe ihn in dein Übungsheft.**

Driving at the age of 16?

[1] As I'm going to be sixteen next month, this question is of great interest to me. **[2]** However, a proposition has been made recently that 16-year-old teenagers should be able to take driving lessons so that they could take their driving test at the age of seventeen. **[3]** In bad weather conditions, driving a motorcycle is dangerous because roads become slippery. **[4]** Many people think that 16-year-old-teenagers are not mature enough to drive. **[5]** Today, German teenagers are allowed to take their driving test at the age of eighteen. **[6]** They are convinced that more accidents would happen if younger people were allowed to drive. **[7]** And on top of all that, public transport can be very lousy at weekends and at night – a car could reduce young people's temptation to hitchhike which is a big danger in itself. **[8]** However, that can be true for older drivers, too: Some people might just never be mature enough to drive. **[9]** I'd like to finish by saying that I hope to be able to take my driving test soon. **[10]** Furthermore, 16-year-olds are already allowed to take a driving test on motorcycles – which are much more dangerous than cars. **[11]** On the one hand I must admit that they are partly right – not every 16-year-old really is mature enough. **[12]** Motorcycles only have two wheels, thus *(somit)* the driver needs a good sense of balance. **[13]** Therefore, driving a car would be the better – and less dangerous – alternative. **[14]** For example, a lot of harm is done by people who drink and drive – alcohol makes driving dangerous, no matter how old someone is.

Richtige Reihenfolge der Sätze:

____

____

4 **Höre dir den Text auf Track 10 der CD zweimal an.**

10

5 **Beantworte die folgenden Fragen zu dem Text aus Übung 4 in deinem Übungsheft.**

a) What is the text about?

b) What's the name of the film that is mentioned in the text?

- ☐ *Freddie and the Chocolate Factory*
- ☐ *Charlie and the Chocolate Factory*
- ☐ *Charlie's Angels*

c) Which teenage dream has come true for Freddie ?

- ☐ acting alongside Johnny Depp
- ☐ eating a lot of chocolate on the set
- ☐ finding a golden ticket

d) What conclusion is drawn at the end?

6 **Höre dir den Text auf Track 11 der CD zweimal konzentriert an. Schlage bei Bedarf nach dem ersten Hören die folgenden Wörter in deinem Wörterbuch nach und schreibe deren Bedeutung auf, bevor du einen zweiten Durchgang machst. Du darfst dir auch weitere Notizen machen.**

11

located – peninsula – vast – orchards – blossom – troubled – graduates – US forces – obtain – research – sources – establish – research department – advice – recover – suffer – despite – semiconductors

7 **Welche Textsorte ist „Silicon Valley"? Begründe deine Antwort in ein oder zwei Sätzen in deinem Übungsheft.**

8 **Beantworte die folgenden Fragen zu dem Text aus Übung 6 (auf Track 11) in ganzen Sätzen.**

a) Where is Silicon Valley?

____

____

b) What could you find there at the beginning of the 20th century?

____

____

c) Where was the US industry concentrated?

____

____

d) Where did the name "Valley of Heart's Delight" come from?

____

____

e) Where did Fred Terman work?

____

____

f) What were the United States Forces interested in? Why?

____

____

g) What did Terman advise his students to do?

h) What does Hewlett-Packard produce?

i) What can you find in the industrial park which Terman created?

j) Where does the name "Silicon Valley" come from?

9 **Höre dir den Text noch einmal aufmerksam an und schreibe eine kurze Charakterisierung von Fred Terman (vier bis fünf Sätze).** 11

10 **Lies den folgenden Text über die Sicherheitshinweise zu einem Mini-Hi-Fi-System durch und unterstreiche die *keywords*.**

- Before operating the system, check that the operating voltage indicated on the type plate of your system is identical with the voltage of your local power supply. If not, please consult your dealer. The type plate is located at the rear of your system.
- When the system is switched on, do not move it around.
- Place the system in a location with adequate ventilation to prevent internal heat build-up in your system.
- The system incorporates a built-in safety feature that prevents overheating.
- Do not expose the system to excessive moisture, rain, sand or heat sources.
- Under no circumstances should you repair the system yourself, as this will invalidate the warranty!
- If the system is brought directly from a cold to a warm location, or is placed in a very damp room, moisture may condense on the lens of the CD unit inside the system. Should this occur, the CD player will not operate normally. Leave the power on for about one hour with no disc in the system until normal playback is possible.
- Electrostatic discharge may cause unexpected problems. See whether these problems disappear if you unplug the AC power cord and plug it in again after a few seconds.
- To disconnect the system from the power supply completely, remove the AC power plug from the wall socket.

11 **Suche die passenden englischen Wörter aus dem Text. Benutze kein Wörterbuch.**

Spannung:	________________	Stromversorgung:	________________
beinhalten:	________________	Standort:	________________
Wiedergabe:	________________	Wandsteckdose:	________________

12 **Finde die Synonyme und Antonyme (Gegensätze) der angegebenen Wörter. Achtung: Der Kontext hilft dir dabei!**

	synonym	**antonym**
at the rear of	______________	______________
to switch on	______________	______________
to prevent	______________	______________
to expose	______________	______________
to invalidate	______________	______________
a damp room	______________	______________

13 **Vervollständige die Sätze, indem du eigene Wörter benutzt. Lies die Sicherheitsanweisungen noch einmal, falls nötig. Schreibe in dein Heft.**

If your system is not identical with the voltage of your own power supply, ...
The system shouldn't be moved around ...
The system should also not be placed in a location ...
If you don't want the guarantee to become invalid, don't ...
If moisture condenses on the lens of the CD, ...

14 **Beantworte die folgenden Fragen. Verwende keine Zitate aus dem Text. Schreibe in dein Übungsheft.**

a) What should you do before you want to use the system?
b) What is a built-in safety feature good for?
c) What may happen if you bring the system from a cold to a warm location?
d) In what situations won't the CD player operate normally?
e) How can you disconnect the system from the power supply?

10.2 Texte zusammenfassen

Das *summary*

Ein *summary* ist die stark gekürzte Fassung eines Textes und beschränkt sich auf die Wiedergabe der **wichtigsten Fakten.** Sie gliedert sich in **Einleitung** *(introduction)*, **Hauptteil** *(main part)* und **Schluss** *(conclusion)*.
Bei Sachtexten benutzt man das *present tense*.

15 **Lies den folgenden Text durch und beantworte die anschließenden Fragen.**

Looking for an answer?
If you're looking for answers, look no further. Our new encyclopedia, the "Encyclopedia 2009", sets new standards:
300,000 headwords, 40,000 visual elements such as colour photos, charts and diagrams, more than 20,000 biographies of important people fill more than 24,000 pages, so our "Encyclopedia 2009" can be called the biggest encyclopedia ever.
With over 125 years of experience and expertise, only the "Encyclopedia 2008" offers its readers an incomparable depth and breadth of various kinds of information. Whether you're up for only a quick access about something that just slipped out of your mind or whether you're interested in detailed articles on almost any imaginable subject, we're here to answer your question!
All entries have been thoroughly revised and updated, and more than 30 % of our articles inform you about new technologies, modern innovations and recent inventions in fields such as nanotechnology and modern genetic research. The 30 volume edition comes with an additional audio-DVD containing high-quality recordings of musical masterpieces, political speeches as well as examples of animal sounds such as the song of the humpback whale etc.
There's almost no information that you won't find in our "Encyclopedia 2009" – don't hesitate and ensure your own access to first-class, up-to-date knowledge now!

a) What kind of text is it?

b) What is the text about?

c) Who is responsible for that text?

d) Where could you read such a text?

e) Why is it written?

16 **Schreibe ein *summary* des Textes in dein Übungsheft.**

17 **Höre dir den Text auf Track 12 der CD zweimal an. Verfasse dann drei bis fünf Sätze in deinem Übungsheft, mit denen du ihn zusammenfasst.**

12

Die *topic outline*

Bevor du das *summary* verfasst, kannst du zu den einzelnen Abschnitten eine Überschrift suchen oder eine **Übersicht der Themen** anfertigen.

18 **Lies den folgenden Text sorgfältig durch. Markiere die wichtigsten Informationen und verfasse eine *topic outline* in deinem Übungsheft.**

Meg Stevens, London

I'm a teenager of seventeen. My teenage years haven't really been as good as they could have been; they are over now because I have a baby daughter and I'm a single mother. By the time my six-month-old daughter will be able to look after herself, I'll be thirty-something, too old to do things that I am now missing out on. I would love to go clubbing and be like all the other teenagers enjoying themselves: unfortunately, I'll never have these things but I'm the one to be blamed – it's all my fault. I should have taken something to prevent getting pregnant. I got pregnant by my first boyfriend – just imagine. He didn't want the baby, but I wouldn't have an abortion. I was terribly scared. My boyfriend wouldn't marry me, of course. He wanted to be free, and above all, his parents disapproved. He simply said, "I don't want to listen to a screaming baby all day long. There is more in life than wasting my time on a baby."

I got used to the idea after a while, and I couldn't wait to put the clothes I'd bought on the baby. My boyfriend didn't care at all – he bought her nothing whatsoever. I never really thought about what it would be like to stay in every night while I was expecting; I was so used to going out almost every night. She's born now, and I love her, but I do wish that I were still free. Before I was pregnant, I still went to school – I was in my last year. I hated being a pupil, but now I think what a pity that I haven't done my A-levels yet. I wish I could do it right now. Maybe I'll never pass them, and I always wanted to go to university; I'd like to become a doctor – one day. If I had the choice to go back in time, I would, and I'd make sure I didn't get pregnant this time. I would have a baby when I was married, but I'd want to be at least twenty-six years old.

19 **Formuliere die markierten Satzteile um, indem du eigene Worte verwendest.**

a) I would be like other teenagers enjoying themselves.

b) I should have taken something to prevent getting pregnant.

c) His parents approved.

d) My boyfriend didn't care at all.

e) I was so used to going out almost every night.

f) I think it's a pity that I haven't done my A-levels yet.

20 **Vervollständige die Sätze in deinem Übungsheft mit eigenen Worten. Benutze die Informationen aus dem Text, aber übernimm sie nicht wörtlich.**

a) Meg is quite frustrated because ...
b) One reason for her frustration is the fact ...
c) Unfortunately her ex-boyfriend ...
d) To make matters worse ...
e) Having no proper school degree, ...

21 **Fasse den Text über Meg in einem *summary* zusammen. Vergiss nicht, dich um einen guten Stil zu bemühen. Schreibe in dein Übungsheft.**

22 **Lies den folgenden Text aufmerksam durch und unterstreiche die wichtigsten Fakten.**

Hi, my name is Laura, and I will be finished with high school in exactly three days. After that I'm free – no looking back. I am seventeen – well, almost eighteen – and have everything to live for. For the eight months before I go to university, I'll have more time on my hands than I'll know what to do with. Maybe I'll tour around Europe. Or perhaps I can travel through America. The possibilities are endless.
I told my parents I wanted to see Vancouver, India and Tibet. I want to see oceans and mountains – jungles and deserts. My mother simply said "fine", as long as I didn't mind being raped and murdered. The world isn't the same as it used to be, she said.
This is it! This is the real thing – I'm not going to waste my time planning for something bigger and better that I'm not even sure will come along. It seems like everything is a preparation for something else. You go to elementary school to prepare for high school. You go to high school to prepare for university. You go to university to prepare for God knows what. Oh yes, I remember – to learn how to make as much money as quickly as possible and finally you can retire at the age of 65 and play tennis and golf all day long. I don't want to end up looking back on my life like this. My father also wondered where I intended to get the money for university once I've spent it on "senseless" journeys and expeditions. And if I didn't decide to go to university, how would I get a job, raise a family, retire? All those tedious questions – I'm simply fed up with them. So here's my suggestion: plan for the future – but only plan for what makes you happy. Not your parents, nor society, and even not your friends. Travel, enjoy yourself, explore. Be purposeless and spontaneous and creative and innovative and free – but make it mean something. Find your own way and when you're retired and old and gray you'll be able to say, "I haven't regretted anything so far."

23 **Setze die Wörter aus dem Wortspeicher richtig in die Sätze ein.**

uncertain – to consider – make the most – adolescent – trying out – tedious routine – mature

Laura is an ____________________ girl who is most ____________________ what to do with her life before she goes to university. She feels like ____________________ several things, such as travelling the world. Her mother, however, asks her ____________________ those plans since the world has become rather dangerous, especially for young women. But how can Laura possibly ____________________ if she avoids risks and difficult situations? She doesn't want to end up like most people, instead she wants to ____________________ of her life. Laura is eager to escape a life full of ____________________.

24 **Beantworte die folgenden Fragen zu Laura. Schreibe vollständige Sätze in dein Übungsheft.**

a) What is Laura's dilemma?
b) How does Laura's mother react to Laura's plans?
c) What about her father? How does he react?
d) What does Laura want to avoid?
e) What does Laura suggest in the end?

25 **Fasse den Text über Laura in eigenen Worten zusammen. Schreibe dein *summary* in dein Übungsheft.**

10.3 Erzählende Texte bearbeiten

Arten von erzählenden Texten

Zu den erzählenden Texten *(narrative texts)* zählt man u. a. den **Roman** *(novel)*, die **Kurzgeschichte** *(short story)*, die **Novelle** *(novella)*, die **Fabel** *(fable)* und das **Märchen** *(fairy tale)*.

26 **Lies den folgenden Ausschnitt aus *Junk* von Melvin Burgess sorgfältig.**

Gemma

My parents are incompetent. They haven't got a clue. They think being a parent is like being an engineer or something – you do this, you do that, and this is the result you get at the other end.

Someone ought to give parents lessons before they allow them to breed.

That night in the garage, we never did anything. I mean, I wanted to sleep with him. It would have been a nice way to say goodbye, and poor Tar could've done with a nice goodbye, really. That's to say, if I'd done it before, it would have been a nice way to say goodbye, but I don't know if the first time is the right way to say goodbye. But I might have done it anyway – for me, for him. It wasn't for either of us I didn't. I only didn't do it for my parents. I wanted to be able to say, Look ... this was my boy-friend. He was in some really nasty trouble, he was really upset, he was hurt, he'd been beat up by his dad for the nth time, he was running away and I spent the night with him because he needed some company.

And I think he might be in love with me. But there was no sex, we never did that. It was just ... being close. Is that human or what?

The only thing I regret is that I put my dad before Tar. I won't make that mistake twice.

When I got home the next day, all hell broke loose.

My dad was wagging up and down the room. "There must be limits ... there must be rules!"

Mum was sitting on the edge of the chair with no lips trying not to cry.

"We all have to follow the rules, Gemma. When I forbid something I expect you to obey me ..."

I tried to smile at my mum but she looked the other way. Then he came

out with this real beauty. Listen to this: "Her reputation is a girl's greatest asset ..."
Stone Age!
"'What about her GCEs?" I said. "What about her ability to put her lipstick on properly?"
My mum tried to bring the conversation into the real world.
"Darling, you're so young –" she began.
"She'll have to learn!"
"What are we going to do, Gemma? Your father's right, there have to be rules. Surely you can see that?"
"Where's David?" my father said. That's Tar. I christened him Tar, because he was always telling me off for smoking.
"You'll get a tar in your lungs," he kept saying.
"Ring up his house and find out," I told my dad.
"I have. He's not at home. But his father's promised to give him what for when he does."
I nearly said, He'll have a long wait, then. But I bit my tongue. "He already has," I told him. "He beat him up again the night before last."
Dad snorted. "He got into another fight, you mean."
Tar's dad's a teacher at one of the local high schools. You can see the way my dad's brain works. Teacher = good. Bad relationship with Tar = Tar's fault.
"He hits the bottle," I told him. "Go round and see him next time. You'll smell it. That's the sort of influence we young people have to look up to," I said.
"Don't try and be clever with me!"
"Look ... Tar was upset. He just needed someone to stay with him. But there was no sex. Honest. All right?"

27 **Lies den Text in Übung 26 noch einmal und konzentriere dich dabei auf den *point of view* des Autors. Vervollständige dann die folgenden Sätze mit den angegebenen Wendungen. Schreibe sie in dein Übungsheft.**

mood and talent permit – first-person narrator – the characters – emotional account of the events – limited in her knowledge – can't be fully trusted – point of view – feelings, thoughts and motives

a) The excerpt at hand is narrated by one of ...
b) The author uses the ...
c) The narrator makes us see everything from her ...
d) Thus the narrator is rather ...
e) The reader only gets to know the narrator's ...
f) The first-person narrator only understands what her ...
g) Being rather limited in her perspective, the narrator in the text ...
h) In the text at hand, the narrator gives the readers an ...

28 **Welche dieser Behauptungen über die Hauptfigur sind wahr, welche falsch? Korrigiere die falschen: Schreibe die richtige Antwort in dein Heft.**

	true	false
a) Gemma is the protagonist.	☐	☐
b) She is a flat character.	☐	☐
c) Gemma is characterized explicitly.	☐	☐
d) Gemma's relationship with her parents is quite a close and friendly one.	☐	☐

29 **Beantworte die folgenden Fragen mit ganzen Sätzen. Schreibe in dein Übungsheft.**

a) What is the main theme in the extract at hand?
b) Describe Gemma's attitude towards her parents.
c) Whose point of view is presented? What is the effect of this choice?
d) How is Gemma presented? What are her basic traits?

30 **Lies folgenden Ausschnitt aus der Short Story *The German Boy* von Ron Butlin und versuche, ohne Wörterbuch so viel wie möglich zu verstehen.**

The woman I can see standing outside in the pouring rain reminds me of Klaus, the German boy. It is the expression on her face: she looks ... so desolate, so utterly unloved. People hurry past her as quickly as possible; if someone does smile, I watch her hesitate for a moment. Then she looks away. [...] At one time I might have pitied her, for that kind of cruelty comes easiest of all. Believe me, I know – Klaus taught me that.
This morning I have come to the office and done nothing. There is a pile of correspondence for me, some of it marked "urgent". Instead I stand and stare out of the window at the well-dressed woman opposite. She is in her mid-forties. I think she is crying but it is difficult to tell at this distance. She has glanced in my direction so I will move back from the window.
I remember my headmaster talking to us before Klaus was brought in. "There is nothing special about him," he said. "Remember, he is just like the rest of us."
When he came into the classroom for the first time, however, it was quite obvious he was not like the rest of us: Klaus looked different, he talked different and, even though he wore the same clothes as us, somehow he seemed to be dressed differently. Everyone looked at him and he looked at the floor. He had fair hair, very pale skin and was quite tall. His shoulders were trembling – an action his long arms increased proportionally, making his hand jerk as if they were receiving a series of small electric shocks.
"This is Klaus, he is going to join your class." The headmaster was a small red-faced man who always looked as if he was too small and too red-faced to be comfortable. When he died a few years later from sunstroke I imagined him as having simply exploded one very hot afternoon. [...]

Klaus didn't even glance at the class he was about to join. He looked more uncomfortable than ever […]. Klaus sat next to me. He didn't speak English but we managed somehow in Latin. He told me he had been born and brought up in Germany but when his father died his mother had married an Englishman. He had only been here a week but he liked it. He said that he and I were friends – *amici sumus*. That was nearly twenty years ago. […]
On his first night in our dormitory Klaus was given the bed next to mine and I could hear him crying. The room was in darkness but I could just make him out under the blankets. He was kneeling and bending forwards with his head pushing into the pillow.
"Klaus, Klaus," I called in a low voice. Quietly I went over to him and sat on his bed.
"Don't cry, don't cry. You're here now. It will be good – you and me together. Honest."
He made some reply in a voice muffled as much by his tears as by the blankets. He probably hadn't understood a word I had said. I sat with him for nearly half an hour while he cried, then I went back to bed. The next night was the same, and every night afterwards. During the day he was fine: he worked hard in class and joined in the games. Gradually his English improved. Each night however, he cried himself to sleep. Then one day, during the morning break, he told me that from then on he was going to speak only in German – except to me, of course. At first I thought he was joking, but he wasn't. […]
He came back afterwards but still refused to speak English. A few days later he was sent home. I have never seen him since and hardly ever given him a moment's thought until now.
It has stopped raining. The woman is still waiting there but in the sunlight, she looks less miserable. She has been there for forty minutes now, at least. […]

31 Kennzeichne die Passagen im Text, die in der Vergangenheit spielen *(flashback)* und diejenigen, die in der Gegenwart spielen. Dann fasse die jeweiligen Abschnitte in deinen eigenen Worten zusammen. Schreibe in dein Übungsheft.

32 Beschreibe die Funktion und die Charakterzüge der Protagonisten der Short Story in Übung 30.

"I"	Klaus

the woman	the headmaster

10.4 Dramatische Texte bearbeiten

Arten von dramatischen Texten

Zu den dramatischen Texten *(drama)* zählt man das Schauspiel allgemein *(play)*, die Tragödie *(tragedy)*, die Komödie *(comedy)*, den Einakter (Kurzdrama) *(one-act play/short play)* und das epische Drama *(epic theatre)*.

33 **Lies den folgenden Text und versuche, so viel wie möglich zu verstehen.**

Fatal Beatings

(Schoolboy music. A formal looking tweedy gentleman with an Edinburgh accent sits at a desk. There is a knock on the door.)

Headmaster: Come in!!!

(*A tidy, sports-jacketed man enters.* Mr Perkins.) *Perkins:* Ah, good morning, Headmaster.

Headmaster: Ah. Mr Perkins. It was good of you to come in. I realize that your're a busy man, but I didn't feel that we could discuss this matter over the electric telephone.

Perkins: No, absolutely, Headmaster, I mean if Tommy's in some sort of trouble I'd like to nip it in the bud.

Headmaster: Well, quite frankly, Mr Perkins, Tommy is in trouble. Recently his behaviour has left a great deal to be desired.

Perkins: Oh, dear me.

Headmaster: Yes, he takes no interest in school life whatsoever, he refuses to muck in on the sports field and it's weeks since any master received any work from him. [...] Quite frankly, Mr Perkins, if he wasn't dead, I'd have him expelled. [...]

Perkins: Tommy's dead?

Headmaster: Yes, he's lying upstairs in sick bay now, stiff as a board and bright green. And this is, I fear, typical of his current attitude. I have pleaded with him, and so has matron, and he will make no effort. [...]

Perkins: How did he die?

Headmaster: Well: it's all got to do with the library. You see we've had some trouble recently with boys taking library books without library cards. Your son was caught and I administered a beating, during which he died. But you'll be glad to know that the ringleader has been caught, so I don't think we'll have to worry about library discipline any more. You see the library-card system ... [...]

Perkins: Exactly what happened? [...]

Headmaster: Oh, that, oh well, one moment he was bending over, and the next he was lying down.

Perkins: Dead?

Headmaster: Deadish. Really, Mr Perkins, I'm starting to find this morbid fascination of yours with your son's death slightly disturbing. What we're talking about here is your son's attitude, and quite frankly I'm beginning to see where he gets it from.

Perkins: At least I never beat him to death. Are you completely mad?

Headmaster: Yes, I'm absolutely furious. In order to accommodate the funeral we've had to cancel afternoon school on Wednesday. I'm sorry, I have to be going.

Perkins: This is preposterous.

Headmaster: Yes it is. Or rather would be – if it were true.

Perkins: What?

Headmaster: I've been joking, Mr Perkins. Forgive me, it's my strange Hibernian sense of humour. I've been having you on.

Perkins: Oh. Thank God for that.

Headmaster: I wouldn't cancel afternoon school to bury that little twerp.

34 **Lies die folgenden Aussagen und unterstreiche die richtige Antwort.**

a) The text at hand is a short play/short story.

b) Ben Elton and Richard Curtis, who wrote the text, are novelists/playwrights.

c) The text in brackets/in italics at the beginning is called description/stage directions.

d) The *desk* and the *door* mentioned in the brackets are parts of the scenery/stage properties.

e) Mr Perkins and the Headmaster are characters/actors.

f) The conversation between Mr Perkins and the headmaster is called aside/dialogue.

g) The text is meant to be performed on stage/turned into a film.

35 **Fülle diese Tabelle in deinem Übungsheft aus. Charakterisiere die beiden Protagonisten aus *Fatal Beatings*.**

characters	outward appearance	words/ thoughts/ behaviour	feelings/ attitudes	other important details
headmaster				
Mr Perkins				

36 **Schreibe mithilfe deiner Notizen aus Übung 35 eine Charakterisierung der beiden Protagonisten, des Direktors und Mr Perkins, in dein Übungsheft.**

37 **Fasse den Inhalt des Textes in etwa sechs Sätzen zusammen. Beginne mit "In the short play *Fatal Beatings* by Ben Elton and Richard Curtis ..." Schreibe in dein Übungsheft.**

10.5 Lyrische Texte bearbeiten

Arten von lyrischen Texten

Lyrische Texte/Gedichte *(poems)* unterscheiden sich von narrativen und dramatischen Texten durch ihre äußere Form (Verse und Strophen). Lyrische Texte sind u. a. **Balladen** *(ballads)*, **Sonette** *(sonnets)*, **Kinderreime** *(nursery rhymes)*, ***limericks*** oder ***songs***.

38 **Lies das folgende Gedicht sorgfältig durch und versuche, es ohne die Hilfe eines Wörterbuches zu verstehen.**

Cinema Poetry
Movies excite me
Whenever I see
Gunfire, dead people,
Growling, and glee.

And I love it when
Heros are winning the fight
And the villain dies slowly
And, yes, in full sight.

And the blood never stops
Flowing over the screen
And the audience trembles
And can't hold a scream.

But I don't like people kissing.

39 **Beantworte die folgenden Fragen zu dem Gedicht in deinem Übungsheft.**

a) How is the poem structured?
b) What can you say about the rhyme scheme?
c) Can you spot any stylistic devices? If you can't name them, simply describe them.

40 **Lies die folgenden Aussagen über den Sprecher des Gedichts. Kreuze diejenigen an, die dir zutreffend erscheinen.**

a) He/she is fascinated by violence. ☐

b) Cruel and horrifying scenes excite him/her. ☐

c) He/she likes watching romantic love stories. ☐

d) He/she enjoys seeing other people suffer. ☐

e) He/she likes being confronted with people kissing. ☐

f) He/she finds love and affection frightening. ☐

41 **Ersetze folgende Zeilen des Gedichts mit Wendungen aus dem Kasten.**

they cry out – it's a pleasure when – the people watching shake – I detest people kissing

I love it when ≈ ______________________________

they can't hold a scream ≈ ______________________________

the audience trembles ≈ ______________________________

I don't people kissing ≈ ______________________________

42 **Erstelle eine Liste der Dinge, die der Sprecher des Gedichts mag und nicht mag. Wie viele Zeilen benutzt er jeweils? Schreibe in dein Übungsheft.**

The speaker likes it when ...
He doesn't like it when ...

43 **Mache dir die Struktur des Gedichts deutlich, dann erläutere anhand seines Inhalts die Begriffe *antithesis/contrast*. Schreibe in dein Übungsheft.**

1 Substantive und Artikel

1 My favourite hobby is hockey. Two **coaches** train our team (...). On Saturdays we usually play two **matches.** In each team there are eleven **players** and we all have hockey **sticks.** Our players wear **green T-shirts** and we all have special **shoes.**
A lot of **friends** and **families** come to watch the matches. (...) I usually eat two or three **sandwiches** and drink two small **bottles** of coke. (...) mother brings two big **cakes.** (...)
What are your **hobbies?**

2 a) friends, windows; beds, bananas
b) houses, oranges; cages, watches
c) books, chocolates, shops, snakes

3 man → men; sandwich → sandwiches; baby → babies; boy → boys; woman → women; class → classes; child → children; knife → knives; box → boxes; potato → potatoes; house→ houses; tooth → teeth

4 a) Your new glasses are nice.
b) My homework was easy.
c) Where are my jeans?
d) I don't have a pair of scissors.
e) Peter has got two pairs of blue trousers.

5 a) Do you really want to wear **some jeans?**
b) Where did you get **these** fantastic headphones?
c) **Many** thanks for your help.
d) You can always buy **another** pair of shorts.
e) Where **are** my pyjamas? – I think I've already packed **them.**
f) £ 15 for **a pair of scissors! They are** really expensive.

6 a) *falsch. Richtig:* Do you want some coffee/a cup of coffee?
b) *richtig*
c) *falsch. Richtig:* Sarah drinks water/some water/a bottle/a glass of water every day.
d) *richtig*
e) *richtig*
f) *falsch. Richtig:* We need some milk/a bottle of milk and four eggs.
g) *falsch. Richtig:* Would you like some bread/a slice of bread?

7 a) I need a new pair of tights/some tights and a pair of pyjamas.
b) There are a lot of people in the park today.
c) Does Liz usually wear glasses/a pair of glasses?
d) My family drinks/drink several bottles of water every day.
e) I would/I'd like to have some chocolate and some bread.

8 a) Lucy's books; b) the Johnsons' car; c) the pupils' teacher; d) Mr Smith's son; e) the colour of your eyes; f) the family's TV; g) the end of the match

9 the boy's class → the boys' class; the school's buildings → the schools' buildings; the man's job → the men's job; the girl's room → the girls' room; the child's toys → the children's toys; the woman's hair → the women's hair; the family's cars → the families' cars

10 (...) My two **brothers** Tim and Joe also have their own rooms. But my two **sisters** share a big room. My **sisters'** room is next to mine and my **parents'** bedroom (...). My **brothers'** rooms are downstairs. **Blacky's** basket is (...) next to Tim and **Joe's** room, so he (...). My **dad's** office and my **mum's** reading room (...) enough for my **parents'** car, my **brothers'** bikes and the **children's** toys.

11 a) Life in England wasn't easy (...), not even **the** life of a king or queen.
b) **The** school that I go to (...). I don't like big schools. Well, I don't like school anyway, but my parents think that school is important (...).
c) **The** people who live in our street are usually very loud. People can be so unfriendly.
d) (...) She goes to university (...). **The** prison is not far from **the** university.

12 a) Bill takes **a** bath every morning and has cornflakes for breakfast.
b) Jenny can't go to school today. She has got **a** headache and **a** temperature.
c) Poor Tim. He broke his leg after breakfast.
d) Jane likes music. In **the** afternoons she often plays **the** guitar.
e) We ususally go on holiday in July.
f) What **a** lovely day! The sun is shining (...).
g) Janet wants to become **a** teacher.

13 I have never eaten **such a lovely meal.**
Look at these clothes. **What a beautiful dress.**
Tim, you must be more careful. It was **quite a stupid thing to do.**
It was raining heavily, but **half an hour later** it stopped suddenly.

We can do our homework quickly. It is **such an easy question.**
A penknife is **quite a useful thing** because you can take it everywhere.

2 Pronomen

1 Hi, my name is Sue. **I** am eleven years old. (...) **He** is 40 years old. (...) **She** is 36 years old. **They** are both teachers. **I** have two brothers. **They** are six and eight years old. (...) but **we** have a nice garden. **It** is quite big. **We** can play football there. **You** can visit me here! **You** are always welcome.

2 a) them; b) her; c) him; d) it; e) us; f) them

3 a) his bike; b) her shoes; c) their basketball; d) its saddle; e) her diary

4 Carole is looking for **her** shoes. **Her** brother is (...). They are looking in **their** bedrooms and in **their** parents' bedroom, but they can't find them anywhere. Carole tells **her** mother: "We're looking for **my** shoes!" – "Ask **your** grandpa. He's in **his** room. (...)."

5 *Mr Simpson:* "Hi Tom. How was the first day at **your** new school?"
Tom: "Hi dad, **my** new school (...) and **our** classroom is nice, too. **It is** a big room (...). **Its** windows are (...)."
Mr Simpson: "Oh dear. Are **your** new teachers so boring?"
Tom: "Well, **our** English teacher (...) is nice. **Her** two sons are in **my** class as well. **Their** table is next to **mine.**"

6 a) them; b) ours; c) his leg; d) your teacher; e) yours; f) its cheese; g) her bag

7 (...) *Mrs Rose:* "Sure. Would you like **these** new potatoes here or **those** sweet potatoes over there?"
Hannah: "**These** new potatoes, please. Are **these** apples sweet?"
Mrs Rose: "Oh, they're okay. But **those** apples over there are lovely."
Hannah: "(...) and **that** watermelon over there. What is **this** round fruit here?"
Mrs Rose: "Oh, **this** is a mango (...)."
Hannah: "(...) And I'll also have a few of **those** bananas over there."

8 a) himself; b) myself; c) themselves; d) ourselves; e) yourselves; f) myself

9 a) We are late, so we must hurry ~~**ourselves.**~~ → ... we must hurry.
b) Be careful, don't cut ~~**you**~~ with that bread knife. → Don't cut yourself with ...
c) (...) He has changed ~~**himself**~~ a lot. → He has changed a lot.
d) My mum always worries when I'm with my friends. → *richtig*
e) Can I get ~~**me**~~ a drink? → Can I get myself a drink?
f) I can't remember ~~**myself.**~~ → I can't remember. I've never (...)

10 a) opens; b) relax – enjoy yourself; c) did ... themselves *(Verstärkung!)*; d) meeting; e) moving; f) help ourselves; g) are ... hiding

11 a) I bought/have bought this book myself.
b) Be careful with the new knife. You can cut yourself.
c) We needn't/don't have to worry.
d) We enjoyed/have enjoyed ourselves very much.
e) Please sit down and don't worry.
f) He hurried because he was afraid in the dark.

12 a) When old friends meet, they often talk to each other.
b) Young and fit people can look after themselves.
c) People who live alone often start to talk to themselves.
d) First she was ill in bed, then he was ill, so they had to look after each other.
e) Fred and Sheila phone every day to help each other with their homework.
f) Please help yourselves. Everything you need is on the table.

13 a) one; b) one; c) ones – ones; d) ones; e) ones

14 a) Friends usually give **each other** presents at Christmas.
b) Anna and I don't see **each other** very often.
c) My brother always cuts his hair **himself.**
d) Stop talking about **yourself.** That's boring.
e) He can't imagine what might happen next.

15 a) Cats clean themselves every day.
b) Mike usually enjoys himself at parties.
c) I don't feel very well at the moment.

d) Pat and Jill understand each other without saying anything.
e) There is a red apple and a green one.
f) Sally's friends often play a game of cards with each other.

3 Adjektive und Adverbien

1 a) as; b) than; c) as; d) than; e) than; f) than; g) as

2 **The longer** you sleep, **the more tired** you get.
The more tired you are, **the more difficult** it is to get up.

3 Dear Pat,
Scotland is great, it is **as nice as** Wales, sometimes I think it is even **more beautiful than** Wales. (...) Yesterday I went climbing. It was **more difficult than** I thought. We had to climb up very high but **not as high as** Snowdon. I was pretty exhausted, almost **as exhausted as** the time we went rowing on the lake. (...) I think pony trekking is **more fun than** mountain biking.
The longer I stay, **the more exciting** it is getting here in Scotland. And the people here are even **friendlier than** back home in Wales. But the summers here seem to be **as cold as** they are in Wales. I hope your holidays aren't **as boring as** they were last year. (...)

4 der Kleine – the little boy/man
die Tote – the dead woman
der Starke – the strong man
ein Kranker – a sick person/man
zwei Schwarze – two blacks
die Weißen – the whites
die Obdachlosen – the homeless
die Schwachen – the weak
die Große – the tall girl/woman

5 a) There are some good programmes for **the young** on TV.
b) There lives **a rich woman** over there (...)
c) **A blind man** was standing at the side (...)
d) The car has just hit **an old man** who (...)
e) Many people have no idea of the problems **the poor** in big cities have.

6 to watch: carefully – more carefully – most carefully
to cycle: well – better – best
to speak: clearly – more clearly – most clearly
to write: badly – worse – worst
to speak: slowly – slowlier/more slowly – slowliest/most slowly
to play: well – better – best
to talk: loudly – more loudly – most loudly

7 a) Betty plays tennis perfectly.
b) John speaks nervously.
c) They read carefully.
d) Christy dances well.
e) It rains heavily in October.
f) You cook fantastically.

8 a) Jenny feels **better than** yesterday but not **well** enough to go to school.
b) Sarah looked around **nervously** and started to speak **quietly.**
c) Bob opened Nasreen's letter **carefully.** It was a **long** letter with **beautiful** handwriting.
d) Mum drives **faster than** dad. She is not **as careful as** dad.
e) The police did a **good** job. They did their job very **well.**
f) Carolyn is an opera singer. She sings **beautifully. As beautiful as** a canary.

9 a) Richard opens his bag slowly.
b) My dad is a careful driver.
c) It is a fast train. It travels very fast.
d) Betty is pretty clever.
e) Harry works very hard. He hardly sleeps.
f) Jim dances very well. He is a good dancer.

4 Verben und Zeitformen

1 It's Monday morning. Sandra usually **goes** to school on weekdays. But today she **is staying** at home because she **has** a bad headache. Mrs Summer usually **works** three days a week in a bookstore. This week, however, she **is working** five days because her boss is on holidays. She **is** just **selling** a book to a woman. Sandra's brother Peter sometimes **writes** a letter to his Grandma. Right now, he **is talking** to her on the phone.
It's Friday. Sandra **is** at school. She **is writing** a maths test at the moment. Sandra **feels** *(Sinneswahrnehmung!)* tired, but she **mustn't go** home yet.
Mrs Summer usually **reads** a book on Saturdays. But today she **is watching** TV because it's the Queen's birthday.
On Sundays Sandra's brother Peter usually **plays** football with his friends. But today they **are playing** hockey instead.

2 we talk: we don't talk, we aren't talking
you run: you don't run, you aren't running
she eats: she doesn't eat, she isn't eating
I come: I don't come, I'm not coming
we start: we don't start, we aren't starting
they play: they don't play, they aren't playing
he drives: he doesn't drive, he isn't driving
it swims: it doesn't swim, it isn't swimming

3 Lily does her homework in her room. But she **doesn't do** her homework in the classroom.
Lily can watch TV in her room. But she **can't/cannot** watch TV in the classroom.
She reads a book in her room every evening. But she **doesn't read** her book in the classroom.
At home, Lily can listen to music. But at school, she **can't/cannot listen** to music.
Lily has got a rug in her room. But she **doesn't have** a rug in the classroom.
Lily likes her room at home. But she **doesn't like** the classroom.

4 a) What time **do you usually get up?**
b) Kim isn't at home. She **is going shopping.**
c) Oh look! It **is snowing** again.
d) Jeff **is still working** on his project in geography.
e) My parents **never eat** in a restaurant.
f) Mary **doesn't take** the dog for a walk on Saturdays.

5 a) Whenever Judy's father **comes** home from work, his daughter **is watching** TV. She **loves** soap operas.
b) Hey, just have a look! Sam **is dancing** again.
c) I **wish** I could stay up here forever.
d) Come on! Let's go home. It **is getting** dark.
e) They **are doing** a lot of hiking these holidays.
f) I **like** that dress you **are wearing** today.
g) To the postman's horror, a big, angry-looking dog **is barking** at him.
h) Don't worry! Our dog **doesn't bite.**
i) Quiet, John, please! Our neighbour **is playing** the piano. He **usually plays** it most beautifully. It simply **sounds** lovely.
j) Jane is terribly cold. She **is shaking** all over.

6 a) It often rains in Ireland.
b) Francis doesn't like going shopping.
c) Bob is always phoning me in the evening.
d) Is/are our team really playing well this summer?
e) The sun is shining, and it is getting hot.
f) Robert gets up, goes to the bathroom, and has a shower.

7 Yesterday Liz and her mother **went** into town. They **took** the bus. On their way they **saw** a car accident. The policemen **were** already there.
Liz and her mother **got off** the bus in front of a big department store. They **bought** two T-shirts and a jacket for Liz.
On their way home, they **stopped** at a supermarket. They **went** in and **got** potatoes and lettuce for dinner. Then they **walked** home and **had** dinner with the whole family.

8 a) Tom and Tina were happy.
b) My family had a big dog.
c) It wasn't very funny.
d) Yesterday we were at home.
e) He had a cold.
f) Last Monday I was ill.
g) Last summer Frank didn't work at the zoo.
h) It was a cold morning.

9 a) was eating; b) entered – was waiting; c) were sitting – opened – came; d) came – was playing; e) was doing – called

10 a) We **met** our friends from California a few years ago while they **were visiting** Europe.
b) Before she **went** out to dinner, she **took** a shower, **painted** her fingernails and **dressed** nicely.
c) Shakespeare **wrote** many theatre plays.
d) Mum **wanted** to know: "What **were you doing** at 11 p.m. last night? You look awfully tired! What time **did you get home** from the party last night?"
e) When I **looked** out of the window last Christmas morning, it **was snowing.**
f) As a girl, I **played** the flute.
g) I **was watching** TV when I suddenly **noticed** a strange smell.

11 a) When did Steve break his arm fooling around in school?
b) Who met her friends in the shopping mall?
c) What was Mum doing when the postman rang?
d) Whom did Sarah write a letter to?
e) When did Lily ride her bike to school every day?

12 Last summer I **had** a frightening experience. At that time I **was travelling** in the USA. I **put up** my tent (...), and I always **slept** very

well. One night, however, while I **was reading** a book in the flickering light of my torch, I **heard** somebody scream. I **closed** my book and **turned** my flashlight off. I **was** just **lacing up** my shoes when I **heard** a terrible snort.
Something enormous **was standing** in front of my tent! I **didn't dare** to breathe. "That might be a bear," I **thought.** Then I **remembered** my whistle. I **blew** the whistle and the bear **disappeared.** I **was still trembling** when I **turned** my flashlight on again and I **did not sleep** well that night.
Next morning, when I **went** into the next village to do some shopping, I **asked** a ranger about bears in national parks. He **told** me (...). I **trembled** again: **had I been having** a dream when I **heard** the screaming and snorting the night before? I **don't know,** but I **decided** to stay in motels for the rest of my holidays.

13 a) Ida's bike is shining. She **has** just **cleaned** it.
b) **Have** you done your homework? – Yes, I **have** already **finished** it.
c) Jim **has had to take** his medicine.
d) Marc **has lived** in Berlin for three years now.
e) We **haven't been** to France yet.

14 Gina has just written a letter.
I have never listened to Indian music.
Harry and Kim have worked in a restaurant for nine months.
We have already been able to book our trip to Paris.
He hasn't been allowed to go to London yet.

15 I have eaten Chinese food since I was ten years old.
Julia and Ron have known each other since 2006.
The girls have talked on the phone for three hours.

16 (...) *Gina Green:* "Mum, dad, wake up! We **have overslept.** I **haven't heard** the alarm clock. Lisa **has just called.** The Sanders **have** already **left.**"
(...) *Dad:* "I **have prepared** the picnic. **Have** you **taken** a shower, Gina?"
Gina: "Yes, I **have just finished** in the bathroom. It's your turn now. **Have** you **packed** (...)?"
Dad: "Yes, I **have put** everything in the bag. But I **haven't found** our swimsuits."
Mum: "I **have just seen** them on the table over there."
Gina: "(...) Lisa **has called** again. The Sanders **have turned** back home because they **have forgotten** their money."

17 a) have you ... bought; b) been; c) have always dreamt; d) has just smashed; e) have been working; f) has the baby been sleeping?

18 Did you sleep well last night?
Did you come to Germany by train?
Have you ever been to Germany?
Have you ever eaten German jelly babies?

19 a) Jim has been playing the piano since he was six years old.
b) We have been preparing a dinner party since 4 p.m.
c) My dad has had his computer since 1990.
d) Amy and Evan have been owning their house for six years now.

20 a) We **have been waiting** for the painters **since** the beginning of the week.
b) The men **have been working** for hours, and they're tired now.
c) Jane **has improved** her English **since** the summer holidays.
d) Jessica seems to be away. I **have been trying** to contact her **for** a week now.
e) Jenny **has sent** me a postcard every week **since** she **is** in Rome.

21 a) After we **had bought** the tickets, we went to the hall.
b) I phoned the police because someone **had stolen** my car.
c) John **hadn't finished** his homework when Peter phoned.
d) **Had** you **gone** to Bristol before you flew to Rome?

22 a) Before Ben went to university, he had left school./After Ben had left school, he went to university.
b) Before the lessons began, the pupils had got to school./After the pupils had got to school, the lessons began./When the pupils got to school, the lessons had already begun.
c) After the train had left, they got to the station./When they got to the station, the train had already left.
d) After the thieves had left the bank, the police arrived./When the police arrived, the thieves had left the bank./Before the police arrived, the thieves had already left.

LÖSUNGEN

e) When the doorbell rang, I had already started breakfast./After I had started breakfast, the doorbell rang./Before the doorbell rang, I had already started breakfast.

23 After Sarah and Sam had decided to marry, they sent out invitation cards.
After they had sent out invitation cards, they looked around for a nice party location.
After they had decided on a meal, they went shopping for a wedding dress and a suit.
After they had everything ready, Sam and Sarah panicked: the idea of having such a big party was simply too much for them.
After they had said sorry to all their friends, the two of them flew to the Caribbean Sea.
After they got married on the beach of a romantic island, they had a wonderful honeymoon.

24 Yesterday, Evan **got up** early and **took** his kids to the zoo. Maya **enjoyed** watching the penguins, and Milo **had** a lot of fun feeding the ducks. After a picnic lunch, Evan **bought** the kids an ice cream. Maya and Milo **were running** around the zoo happily for many hours and **had** a perfect day.
At home, Evan's wife Amy **had** a wonderful day, too. She **enjoyed** the quietness. She **took** a bath. She **read** a book and **took** a nap in the sunshine.
And after so many hours to herself, she **was looking forward to** seeing her family again.

Rückwärts erzählt:
Yesterday, after many hours to herself, Amy was looking forward to seeing her family again.
She had had a wonderful day at home and had enjoyed the quietness. She had taken a bath, had read a book and had taken a nap in the sunshine.
Amy's husband Evan had gotten up early and had taken the kids to the zoo. Maya had enjoyed watching the penguins, and Milo had had a lot of fun feeding the ducks. After a picnic lunch, Evan had bought the kids an ice cream. Maya and Milo had been running around the zoo for many hours. They had had a perfect day, too.

25 "(...) I realized that I **had forgotten** my money. (...) because I **had been looking forward to** it for a few weeks.
So we ran, but when we got to my house, I realized that I **hadn't taken** a key with me either, (...) everybody **had gone** out. (...) opened the door, we **had been ringing** the doorbell (...) we got there the bus **had already left.**
(...) we couldn't get in because the concert **had already begun** – but Emma was worth all the trouble and money I **had spent** on the ticket ..."

26 *Ray:* "(...) My dad **is going to repair** it on Saturday."
Simon: "(...) I **will check** it for you."
Ray: "Thanks, but I need new brakes. Dad and I **are going to buy** them (...)."
Simon: "Yes, of course, I **will come,** too."
Ray: "And what about next Friday? I **am going to play** basketball with Tom and Jerry."
Simon: "I can't. Diana is in hospital, and I **am going to visit** her next Friday."

27 *Michael:* "I am **not going to study** any vocabulary (...). However, I **will be staying** with my girlfriend (...). And as soon as I **will have finished** school next summer, I **will take** her (...)."
Sarah: "I hope it **will be** hot all summer. Then **I'll be** spending all afternoons at the swimming-pool. I assume **I'll get** a good tan then."
Mary: "I **am going to sleep in** all the days. And I**'m going to do** a lot of (...)."
Susie: "My parents and I **are going to spend** two weeks in Greece. I guess we**'ll do** (...)."
Sharif: "I**'m going to redecorate** my room. Maybe I**'ll make** a new shelf. I hope I**'ll have finished** all the work until (...)."
Monica: "We **will be hosting** an exchange student (...). She**'ll be arriving** at London Airport (...). And I **am going to visit** her (...)."
Marc: "I **won't do** anything special. I**'ll just relax and see** what happens."

28 a) will have been married; b) won't have left; c) will have worked

29 a) Our train leaves in 20 minutes. When do we arrive in New Orleans?
b) Next week we are flying to Denver and we are going to stay there for two weeks.
c) Michael will have learnt/learned how to surf during his holidays.
d) When he is 70, he will still be running around.
e) When you arrive, my parents will be waiting for you.
f) The mechanic won't have repaired the dishwasher by Monday.

30 a) will you have finished; b) will have; c) will have done; d) will come; e) will have left; f) will be

31 a) **I'll help you.**
b) **Are you doing** anything tomorrow evening?
c) **I'm going to paint** the fence.
d) What time **does** the last bus **leave?**
e) Hasn't the doorbell just rung? I'll go. → ***richtig***
f) Tom is sure that he **will pass** his final exams.
g) The Queen **will visit** Ascot as in the years before.
h) By the time we arrive, she **will have made** all the sandwiches.
i) Geoffrey will be sixty next June. → ***richtig***
j) It **will possibly be** another boring weekend.

5 Das Passiv

1 a) In Switzerland four languages **are spoken.**
b) Do you know when the post **is usually collected?**
c) Look, Kevin! Your bed **is being made** again.
d) The bins **are always emptied** in the evening. It is 6 p.m. – the bins **are being emptied** now.
e) A lot of apples and pears **are grown** here.
f) The grass **is being cut** at the moment.

2 a) Coffee is just being offered to the guests.
b) Silly stories are often told to me.
c) We are given new English exercises every lesson.
d) Some important information is being told to them.
e) Pete is usually promised a new bike before his birthday.

3 a) We are never told funny jokes by Tim.
b) The tourists are being shown the most interesting sights by the guide.
c) He is never offered a cigarette by John's friends.
d) Her penfriend is sent a long letter by Pat every summer.

4 a) **We** are told very interesting facts in our history lesson.
b) Sandwiches are often given **to him** for dinner.
c) The leaflets **are sent** to the tourists every spring.

5 a) The problem is explained to the pupils (by the teacher). The pupils are explained the problem (by the teacher).
b) Credit cards are accepted (by this shop).
c) Laura was allowed to go to the party (by mum).
d) A bracelet was given to Lisa for Christmas (by John)./Lisa was given a bracelet for Christmas (by John).

6 He is said to be very rich.
It is reported that four people were killed in the accident.
Susie is said to be a good pupil.
The president is thought to make a speech tomorrow.

7 a) Tom **is said** to be very sensitive.
b) (...) **It is reported** that (...).
c) Thousands of children **are believed** to have lost (...).
d) (...) **It is reported** four people were killed.
e) Angelina Jolie **is said** to be pregnant again.

8 The rules must be followed.
The team shirt has to be worn by all team members.
The goal ought to be kept clear by the goalkeeper.
The other team must be stopped from scoring by the defender.

9 a) This door must be kept shut.
b) This film should be forbidden.
c) Helen's bike must be repaired.
d) The new bridge might be opened tomorrow by the President.

10 (...) I **was warmly welcomed** by my new classmates. First, I **was shown** our new classroom. (...) I **was taught** some history of the city, too. And I **was offered** to join (...). I **was quickly accepted** by the teachers, too. I **was asked** a lot of questions.
(...) She, too, **was invited** to join (...). However, we **were told** by (...). But last Saturday, we **were invited** to a big party (...)

11 a) Rubbish is collected by the dustmen.
b) The job had been finished at seven.
c) The house has been sold.
d) You were warned by the police.
e) The winning goal was scored by David Beckham.
f) The film is being shown now.

g) Bob's bike has been stolen.
h) He is always admired.

12 The accident happened between Bath and Bristol yesterday. One crash victim was taken to hospital by an ambulance. An injured woman was pulled from a burning car by passing motorists, but the driver wasn't rescued. The passenger in the Mercedes was taken to hospital, and he is being kept under observation at the moment. The police believe that the driver of the Mercedes lost control on the wet road. Witnesses are being interviewed by the police at present. The motorway has been opened again recently. Since this terrible accident, motorists have been driving more carefully.

13 a) was being taken down; b) was being held; c) were being written; d) was being hauled away

14 We were allowed to organize a trip to New York.
We were advised to book the trip through a travel agency.
We were promised to visit Manhattan.
We were told to be careful.
We were given some use useful information about NYC.
translation:
Es wurde uns erlaubt, eine Kurzreise nach New York zu organisieren.
Es wurde uns empfohlen, die Reise über ein Reisebüro zu buchen.
Man versprach uns, Manhattan zu besuchen.
Es wurde uns gesagt, vorsichtig zu sein.
Man gab uns einige nützliche Informationen über NYC.

15 have taught → have been taught; has taken → has been taken; had sung → had been sung; has treated → has been treated; had kept → had been kept; have put → have been put; had drunk → had been drunk; have seen → have been seen; had painted → had been painted

16 a) Tim has written a poem for Pete's birthday. → A poem has been written for Pete's birthday (by Tim).
b) Somebody had ruined the building. → The building had been ruined (by somebody).
c) Susie the cat has caught many mice over the past years. → Many mice have been caught over the past years by Susie the cat.
d) The teachers have been asking her a lot of questions. → She has been asked a lot of questions by her teachers. / A lot of questions have been asked by her teachers.
e) He hadn't finished reading the newspaper article when the postman rang. → The newspaper article had not been finished reading when the postman rang.
f) Amy has given us an interesting tour through San Francisco. → We were given an interesting tour through San Francisco by Amy. / An interesting tour through San Francisco was given to us by Amy.
g) She hasn't broken her arm in the accident. → Her arm hasn't been broken in the accident.
h) Somebody had told a boring story. → A boring story had been told (by somebody).

17 While the Reynolds were on holiday, their house was broken into by two burglars.
After the windows had been broken, the living room was entered.
A lot of valuable objects were taken by the burglars.
Before the diamonds were stolen, the door of the safe had been opened.
The police were called by Mrs Marble while the house was being cleared out.
While the house was being left, the burglars were arrested by the police.

18 Yesterday a 32-year-old swimmer **was killed** by (...). This terrible accident **happened** near the city of Perth. (...), but after he **had been pulled** out of the water, the heavily injured man **died.** A friend, who **dragged** the victim to the shore, **was bitten** on his legs and feet and **had to be taken** to hospital.
Since last September three men **have become** victims (...). Among others, a 23-year-old surfer **had been pulled** from his surfboard before the tourists **were warned** about the sharks. Some tourists **found** his board, but his body **disappeared** without a trace. Only a few days later, a tourist from England **was attacked** by a shark. Luckily, the young man (...) **survived.** However, he **is being treated** in hospital now. He **is supposed** to fly back to (...). It **is being investigated** what is causing the aggressive behaviour of the sharks.

19 You will be given plenty of water and food.
You will be treated well.
You will be taken to regular check-ups at the vet's.

You will be given extra treats once in a while. And you will be loved by all members of the family!

20 a) will have been completed; b) will have been taken; c) won't have been released

21 a) **Jason** was promised a better salary./A better salary was promised to Jason.
b) **She** was thanked for her hard work.
c) The environment will be talked **about** in the weeks to come.
d) An enormous Valentine card has been sent **to** my brother./My brother has been sent an enormous Valentine card.
e) **Kim** hasn't been shouted **at** since she was a kid.
f) Rivers or lakes mustn't be **used** as dumping grounds for toxic waste.

22 a) The new museum will be opened in April. → Das neue Museum wird im April eröffnet.
b) Her room is being painted at the moment. → Ihr Zimmer wird gerade gestrichen.
c) Yesterday evening we were being watched by a stranger. → Wir wurden gestern Abend von einem Fremden beobachtet.
d) Our cat is fed every day. → Unsere Katze wird jeden Tag gefüttert.
e) She had been promoted because she worked hard. → Sie war befördert worden, weil sie hart arbeitete.
f) All rules must be followed by the team. → Alle Regeln müssen vom Team befolgt werden.
g) The lawn has just been cut. → Der Rasen ist gerade gemäht worden.

6 Modale Hilfsverben

1 a) Last year we **could/were able to** go to India.
b) (...) **Could/Can** you help me with (...)?
c) At the moment Marc **cannot/is not able to** play the bass. But next year he **will be able to** play the bass.
d) Toby **couldn't** ride a bike when he was three. Now he's ten, so he **is able to** ride a bike.
e) **Can/Are you able to** climb Mount Everest?
f) **Could/Can** you speak louder, please?

2 a) You **aren't allowed to** turn left, but you **are allowed to** turn right.
b) She **wasn't allowed** to borrow the skateboard last week.
c) **Were you allowed** to watch TV last week?
d) Dogs **are not allowed** in the cinema.

3 a) The shop assistant couldn't speak a word of English. (Unfähigkeit)
b) The shops on Queens Road could still be open. (Möglichkeit)
c) You can't sit/aren't allowed to sit at this table. (Verbot)
d) Mrs Collins, you can/are allowed to come in. (Erlaubnis)

4 (...) *Betty:* "I feel good today but I **had to** go (...)."
Instructor: "That's alright. Yesterday you **had to** learn (...) tomorrow you **will have to** pass a test. So we **have got to** start right away."
John: "Can we put on our snowboards right now? Or **do we have to** have a warming-up first?"
Instructor: "Of course you always **have got to** do a warming-up first. Today you **have got to** get up the hill (...) what **do you have to** do?"
Steven: "We **have got to** stand (...)." (...)

5 a) (...) I **have got to** do my homework.
b) (...) I **must** drink something.
c) *Mother to Jill:* "Don't be late! You **must** be home at 10 o'clock!" – *Jill to her friends:* "I **have got to** be home at 10 (...)."

6 a) you don't have to go; b) you needn't help; c) you mustn't drink; d) you needn't pay; e) you don't have to go; f) I mustn't stay up

7 a) Shall I open the window?
b) Shall we have something to eat?
c) Shall we have a break?
d) Shall I answer the phone?

8 a) should go home; b) should buy them; c) should look for a cheaper one; d) shouldn't go to work; e) shouldn't eat too much

9 a) My bike is dirty. I must/have got to clean it.
b) Where shall we go on holiday this year?
c) You should do more sport.
d) Shall we meet at 7.30 p.m.?
e) Must you go/Do you have to go to bed early?
f) Did you have to wait long in front of the cinema yesterday?

10 Shall we go hiking in the nearby forest? (...) Perhaps we should/ought to take raincoats with us.

But we shouldn't/oughtn't to walk too far. (...)
Shall we take sandwiches? Shall I make them?
Shall we have a picnic by the lakeside?
We should/ought to take a blanket to sit on.
If we want to go hiking, we shouldn't/oughtn't to get up too late.

11 Lösungsvorschlag:
a) The roads may/might be slippery.
b) Caroline may/might be at home now.
c) I may/might invite Kevin, too.
d) I may/might spend my holidays in Ireland.
e) May/Might I use your telephone?
f) May/Might I borrow it?
g) But I may/might be wrong.

12 a) Will/Would you set the table, please?
b) Will you have some more potatoes?
c) Will/Would you shut the window, please?
d) Will/Would you dial for me, please?
e) Will/Would you help me translate it, please?
f) Will/Would you go for a walk with the dog, please?

13 Lösungsvorschlag:
a) Tracy would like to go to Princeton next year.
b) Tracy's friend won't study. She would like to go abroad first.
Will you tell me about your problem?
c) Will you tell me about your problem?
d) Brian won't admit that he stole the money.

14 (...) *Fiona:* "I expect she **will be** (...)."
Martin: "(...) She **won't want** (...)."
Judy: "(...) She **will meet** her boyfriend (...)."
Martin: "Certainly. And they **will learn** German together."
Judy: "Well, they **won't do** that – (...), but Pam **won't smoke,** I suppose."
Fiona: "(...) However, Pam **won't lie** (...)."
Fiona: "(...) I suppose Tom **will want** to have (...). Her mum **will look forward to** (...)?"

15 a) wouldn't pay attention; b) will listen to music; c) won't stop smoking; d) would sit in a pub and chat with other people; e) would dance

7 Die indirekte Rede

1 The boy says that **he has lost his purse.**
The girl tells Linda that **she can't come to her party.**
My parents explain to me that **they will be home late.**

2 *Sarah:* "I have forgotten to do my homework."
Mr Hall: "My children shouldn't go to parties."
Tim's mother: "You can't have a new computer."

3 Fiona said that she didn't want to do anything.
Beth told me that her friend and she would probably visit some friends in Scotland.
Brian told us that he had already spent his pocket money on comics.
Lucy says that she works at the supermarket every Saturday.
Dave said he might not be at home on Sunday.
Sophie told me that she was ill on Wednesday.

4 a) My cousin said he will meet → **would meet** me in front of the restaurant.
b) Richard told James that he is going to → **was going to** buy a new computer.
c) Mr Dixon said he hasn't been → **hadn't been** to a museum since 2001.
d) George told me that he can help → **could help** with my English homework.
e) Tina said me → **said to me** that her parents had been strict when she was young.

5 a) Jane says that Mary is good at Biology.
b) Mary told me that she would come later.
c) Ann and Michael said that they wanted to go to the cinema at the weekend.
d) Jenny tells her mother that she invited/has invited a friend.
e) Tom said that he had started to play the guitar in 2005.

6 a) said/says; b) said; c) tell; d) tell; e) told; f) say – told

7 a) Jeff told me that Sue was ill.
b) Anne and Michael said they wanted to play tennis.
c) Tom told me that he didn't like tea.
d) Mrs Brown says that she gets up early every day.
e) Julia's parents told her that she couldn't wear this dress for school.

8 Tom said that he would do his homework the next day.
Rachel told her mother that she had seen a wonderful dress at her favourite shop that day.
Paul tells his friend that he is going to go to England on holiday this year.
Gillian asked if/whether I had ever been to the United States.

Meg told her friend that the rain had stopped in the evening the day before.
Rita said that she was going to have her birthday party there.

9 a) The Millers say, "We go out for dinner once a week." → The Millers say that they go out for dinner once a week.
b) Susan says, "I haven't studied my English vocabulary in a while. But we'll be writing a test next week, so I'd better study it tonight." → Susan says that she hasn't studied her English vocabulary in a while. And she adds that they will be writing a test the next week, so she had better study them tonight.
c) Lucy told her friend, "I met a nice boy at the disco last night." → Lucy told her friend that she had met a nice boy at the disco the night before/the previous night.
d) The teacher said, "We will go on a one-week school trip to London next March." → The teacher said that they would go on a one-week school trip to London the following March.
e) Laura states, "Melanie's party this evening starts at 7.30." → Laura states that Melanie's party starts at 7.30 p.m. tonight.
f) Rob says, "I'll buy a new mobile phone next month." → Rob says that he'll buy a new mobile phone next month.
g) Cynthia told her boyfriend, "It's my Chinese grandma's birthday today. She is going to celebrate here in England." → Cynthia told her boyfriend that it was her Chinese grandma's birthday that day and that she was going to celebrate there in England.
h) Helen asked, "I haven't seen Jill's mother today. Where did she go?" → Helen asked where Jill had gone because she hadn't seen her that day.

10 a) hadn't seen; b) is going to play; c) would be enjoying; d) had been; e) was; f) wanted

11 Peter said that I should buy that CD.
Peter said to Mary it would be nice if he could take her out for dinner.
Father said that I needn't pretend to be clever.
Mother told me that I had to/must take care of my sister while she was at the dentist's.
Brian said he could come over and babysit.
My Mum said that it was seven thirty. She said that I wasn't to sleep in.

12 Mother said (that) I mustn't/shouldn't/wasn't to eat so much chocolate.
The bank manager said (that) I had to pay back the money that month.
Peter assumed that Kate must be tired after running the marathon. (*must* bleibt unverändert, da es sich um eine Annahme bzw. Schlussfolgerung handelt!)
The teacher said that I needn't/didn't have to worry about my school report.
Tom said that he was sure he would enjoy his holidays.
The coach said that he might need some help with the junior team.
The sign said that you mustn't/weren't to eat ice cream while riding the tram.
Jane said she might go to Canada next year.

13 a) had had; b) might; c) could; d) would

14 Jack asked what kind of sports competition it had been.
He wanted to know where the competition had taken place.
He asked why there are/were five people in a team.
He wanted to know which distance they had to cover in the race.
He asked who had won the race.

15 Steve asked if/whether I was good at football.
Stacey wanted to know if/whether I had listened to my new CD already.
Ben asked Ken if/whether his parents liked movies.
Evan wanted to know if/whether Bill had ever tried to write a weblog.
Bill asked Andy if/whether he would travel to Germany next summer.
Sara asked me if/whether I liked Mexican food.
Evan asked Amy if/whether she had brought enough crisps for the party.
Mum wanted to know if/whether John had practised enough for her concert.
Mary asked Jodie where she had met her boyfriend for the first time.
Daneesh asked Peter whether/if he would come to Mike's party the following weekend.

16 **Lösungsvorschlag:**
Anne promised to buy me a new book.
Will warned me not to eat too many chillis because they were very hot.
Father threatened to take away my computer if I didn't pass my exam.
Mother told Ryan to lay the table.
Melanie advised me to go and see a doctor.

17 We promise/We are told to be polite to all guests within those premises.
We promise/We are told not to insult other people.
We promise/We are told not to fight with other party guests.
We promise/We are told to help our fellows when necessary.
We promise/We are told not to drink and drive.

8 Der Satz

1 a) Mr Smith usually teaches English and history.
b) Lily sometimes eats cornflakes for breakfast.
c) Many children learn English at school.
d) We sometimes go to the countryside on Sundays.
e) The children never interrupt their teacher.
f) David and Gordon usually play tennis at school on Mondays.
g) Mrs Taylor usually drinks two cups of coffee every morning.
h) The children always do their homework in the afternoon.

2 a) Susie never forgets her homework.
b) We always go swimming on Saturdays.
c) We often eat a lot of ice cream in summer.
d) Our English teacher never forgets to give us some homework.
e) Tina usually goes to the supermarket on Tuesdays.
f) Anne and Amy sometimes visit their mother together.
g) Mr Hope always helps his wife in the evening.

3 a) My parents go to work at 8 o'clock every day.
b) Our teacher travels to Madrid in Spain in summer.
c) Hanna does her homework at the desk in her room.
d) I go shopping in the big shopping-centre in town every Friday.
e) The school bus stops at the bus stop at 7:15 a.m. from Monday to Friday.
f) The children often go swimming at a big sports centre in town in summer.

4 a) The alarm was raised **as soon as** (...).
b) You can have a passenger (...) **provided that** the passenger wears a helmet.
c) I like him, **but** he doesn't like me.
d) **After** I had locked up, I went straight to bed.
e) My sister was ill. She **neither** ate **nor** drank **until** she was well again.
f) We had a great holiday **although** (...).
g) **Supposing that** I lent you my car, (...)?
h) Our old house was (...) **whereas** (...).
i) **When** I saw his face, I knew (...).
j) (...) **Moreover,** she acts **as if** she she (...).

5 a) as soon as; b) although; c) because; d) while; e) as; f) Unless

6 a) I didn't call you since I'd lost your phone number.
b) There was widespread flooding because there was a violent storm last week.
c) After I had been to Boston, I flew to Houston.
d) Supposing we will miss the last train, we will take a taxi.
e) The Johnsons had an alarm system installed so that nobody would break into the house again.

7 a) I bought/have bought this book so that I can improve my English.
b) The children behaved as if nothing had happened.
c) Sarah was careful whereas Christopher made a lot of mistakes.
d) I knew that she would be angry/furious as soon as I saw her face.
e) As long as the weather doesn't get any better, we won't be able to go outside.

8 If I tell you the truth, you will be shocked.
If you don't call her, she will be angry.
If Susan stays longer, she will miss the bus.
If we work hard, we will get good marks.
If he doesn't do his homework, he won't pass the exams.

9 a) I **will be** there **if** you **arrive** at (...).
b) Sally **will read** the book **when** she **gets** it.
c) **When** she **arrives** (...), she **will meet** him.
d) **If** you **make** too many mistakes, you **won't pass** the exam.

10 a) didn't rain; b) didn't have; c) understood; d) were/was

11 a) If I read more, I would be better informed.
b) If Sally lent Pete some money, he wouldn't give it back to her.

c) What would you write your penfriend if you got a letter from him?
d) We could eat together if we met.

12 a) If you **lived** in England, (...).
b) Can you phone me if you **get** to the hotel?
c) John could be happier if he **was** back (...).
d) If you **wait** a minute, I will go with you.
e) If you went by train, it **would be** quicker (...).

13 a) Typ II; b) Typ I; c) Typ I; d) Typ II; e) Typ III

14 a) If it rains, I **will take** my umbrella.
b) I **would close** all schools if I were (...).
c) Would you be glad if I **bought** your old car?
d) If you don't have (...), I **will lend** you one.
e) If he had played a bad concert, his mother **would have been disappointed.**
f) **Would you read** more if you had more time?
g) I couldn't have come today if my father **hadn't lent** me his car.
h) My friends would have laughed at me if they **had seen** me trying to ride a unicycle.
i) Your hair **would look** better if you hadn't cut it.

15 a) If you get married one day, I will play the violin.
b) If Sal had read the book, he wouldn't have gone to see the movie.
c) If you met Brad Pitt, would you ask for an autograph?
d) If my mother hadn't broken her leg, she would have travelled to Italy.
e) If I buy a car, I will buy a convertible.
f) If you read that travel guide, you would know a little more about California.

16 If you are ill, you must go and see a doctor.
I would panic if I found a spider in my bed.
If I were you, I wouldn't meet her again.
If you eat too much, you will get fat.
If you shouldn't like the DVD, I will take it back.

17 a) If this computer wasn't so expensive, my brother would buy it.
b) If you stay at home tonight, we can/will be able to watch that film together.
c) I would have gone to the restaurant with you if I had felt well that day.
d) If there hadn't been so much traffic on the way to the airport, the Millers wouldn't have missed their flight.

18 a) Frederic is a boy **who** can sing and play the guitar.
b) Jason's mother is a nurse **who** works at the hospital.
c) They showed a film **which** was brilliant.
d) This is Margret **whose** aunt works in the bakery.
e) This is my friend Ron **who** bought a blue bike.
f) Mr Harold is the neighbour **whose** dogs are always barking.
g) Mrs Richard is the teacher **who** went to Rome last year.

19 Do you see the bike **that/which** is in front of the shop? → **nR**
This is the boy **who/that** helps me with my homework. → nR
The homework, **which** we got last week, is difficult. → nnR
Elvis Presley, **who** was a famous pop star, died in 1977. → nnR
Have you got a knife **that/which** is sharp enough for the bread? → nR
They stole my wallet **which/that** was in my jacket. → nR
Margaret Thatcher, **who** was called the "Iron Lady", was British prime minister (...). → nnR

20 a) The woman who was opening the door was wearing red jeans.
b) The policeman who stopped my bike was very nice.
c) Sue is wearing an anorak (that) I like.
d) Some pupils took their exams which weren't difficult at all.
e) How much were the apples (which) you bought?
f) You gave me a CD (which) I can't find anywhere.
g) You made this cake which was wonderful.
h) I have got a friend who is very good at repairing computers.

21 a) Is that the girl ~~who's~~ → **whose** photo was in the papers yesterday?
b) That's the hotel ~~at whose~~ → **at which** we stayed.
c) Where is the lady ~~which~~ → **who** lost her purse?
d) Where is the pen ~~with that~~ → **with which** I always write?
e) That's the boy ~~who~~ → **whose** sister is good at French.

22 a) Is that the family **whose son was on TV yesterday?**

b) Where is the computer magazine **which I have just bought?**
c) That's the girl **who I sit next to at school.**
d) The house **that my parents bought** has a garden.

23 a) The house which has blue doors is very big.
b) Drivers who drink a lot of alcohol can be very dangerous.
c) I saw the girl, whose sister is called Mary, in the library yesterday.
d) Jenny cooked a meal which/that she had tasted in Italy.
e) The boy who can play football very well broke his leg.
f) She red a book that her friends had recommended.

24 a) Our school**, which** is located across a wonderful park**,** is old but beautiful.
b) It was my sister **who** gave me tickets for the rock concert.
c) The people I work with are very nice.
d) Last week I took my little niece to the cinema**, which** is just around the corner from where I live.

25 a) The woman who ... → *keine Kommas*
b) Where is the box that ... → *keine Kommas*
c) Mrs Bell, who surprised us all, is a most lovely woman.
d) The teacher spoke ... → *keine Kommas*
e) The Channel Islands, which consist of four main islands, lie in the English Channel.

26 Lösungsvorschlag:
I'll always remember the day I met my girlfriend/boyfriend.
I met somebody whose mother/father is a famous musician.
I got the job which/that I had applied for/for which I had applied.
I don't agree with the opinion (which/that) some people have.
I don't like people who are never on time.

27 a) Sally's boyfriend doesn't even like the idea of Sally becoming a movie star.
b) My sister isn't good at saving money.
c) Laura is already talking of moving out when she's 18.
d) Rick's mom is very fond of him spending a lot of money on books.
e) Samuel is frightened of going to the dentist's again.
f) The girls suggest going out for dinner.
g) Linda's nephew and niece like her reading bedtime stories.

28 a) How about going out for an ice cream this afternoon?
b) I have no difficulties studying English.
c) Are you interested in playing football?
d) Are you thinking of buying a new computer?
e) Some girls are dreaming of becoming a pilot.
f) She has a lot of experience in teaching.

29 a) I can't stand **cleaning** the bathroom.
b) I prefer **going** for a walk to **watching** TV.
c) It is right **to help** the poor.
d) It's not worth **buying** lottery tickets.
e) I was delighted **to hear** that I had won (...).

30 a) The boy playing football is dreaming of a big career.
b) The pool built in our backyard wasn't worth its money.
c) Laura knows the boy living next door very well.
d) Reading a good book, I didn't answer the phone.

31 a) in; b) of; c) for; d) of; e) of; f) before; g) for

32 a) *wrong. Right:* How about **travelling** (...)?
b) *wrong. Right:* I don't have an interest in **studying,** (...).
c) *right*
d) *wrong. Right:* Ian spent a lot of time **trying** (...).
e) *right*
f) *right*
g) *wrong. Right:* She left the house without **eating** (...).
h) *wrong. Right:* It's no use **complaining** about (...).

33 a) It's not worth **buying** that book. (...)
b) My mother forced me **to study** some (...).
c) Dad permitted Hannah **to go** to the party (...).
d) Would you mind **helping** me with the dishes?
e) I can hardly resist **eating** another ice cream.
f) Instead of **watching** TV, you should (...)!
g) Children usually love **to play/playing** games.
h) Cara was the best pupil **to play** the violin.

34 a) Arriving at my friends' house, I was welcomed by their dog.
b) Noticing that the old lady felt sick, Jim called an ambulance.

c) Not having worked in the garden for a while, Jim felt tired after mowing the lawn.
d) Having eaten too much chocolate, Toby felt awful.

35 a) My boyfriend stopped smoking. (he stopped to smoke = er blieb stehen, um zu rauchen)
b) He used to get up early. (he is used to getting up early = er ist es gewöhnt, früh aufzustehen)
c) We tried to find the keys. (we tried finding the keys = wir probierten aus, die Schlüssel zu finden)
d) Letzten Winter habe ich Snowboarden ausprobiert. (I tried to snowboard = ich habe versucht zu snowboarden)
e) I must remember to buy some tea. (I must remember buying ... = ich muss daran denken, wie ich Tee gekauft habe)
f) You forgot meeting Jill, didn't you? (you forgot to meet Jill = du hast vergessen, sie zu treffen)
g) The Prime Minister went on talking about his foreign policy. (the Prime Minister went on to talk = der Premierminister fuhr fort und sprach ... → Themenwechsel)

36 a) Instead of **going out,** you should (...)
b) **The weather being** sunny, Andy decided (...)
c) Feeling hungry, the teenagers ... → ***richtig***
d) It's no use **trying** it again.
e) **On seeing** how dark it was, Timmy ...
f) **The novel being** long and boring, ...

37 a) The dress worn by Cecil must have cost a fortune.
b) Being confused by modern technology, Tom doesn't want to buy a computer.
c) Written in Chinese, the text is quite hard to understand.
d) Not knowing which road to take, we had to ask a resident.
e) Not being able to sleep, Jane got up and walked around.
f) Having completed his work, Mr Taylor went for a walk.

38 a) My parents believe that I get excellent marks by learning more.
b) In spite of learning hard for her finals, Victoria failed them with flying colours.
c) On seeing her sister after all these years, Jill started to cry.
d) Apart from being a talented musician she is also a gifted photographer.

39 a) make – makes; b) Let – lets; c) made – let; d) let – make – let; e) let – make – let

40 a) A terrible noise didn't let me sleep last night.
b) I have my hair cut every month.
c) Why don't you have your motorbike repaired?
d) My parents made me work in the garden last week.
e) Her mother didn't want to let Sue go at first.

41 a) Rarely did Robert stay at home to do school work.
b) Never did he think about what his future might bring.
c) Hardly had he gone to university when he had to work harder.
d) Seldom has he felt so determined to be successful.

42 a) Never had he believed any stories about this fascinating city.
b) Neither had he seen any skyscrapers because he came from a small town.
c) Hardly could he believe his eyes when he saw the Empire State Building.
d) Had you told me about your problems, I could have helped you.
e) Should you happen to be around, come and see us.

43 a) Such **was the force of the wind** that (...).
b) So **serious was the famine** that (...).
c) Such **was the power of the punch** that (...).
d) So **strange did his story sound** that (...).

44 a) My parents would never treat me so badly.
b) He had seldom seen such a sunset.
c) If this should not work, ask somebody to help you.
d) Jane not only wanted to go out with Burke, but she even phoned him twice a day.

9 Wortschatz

1 um drei Uhr – **at** three o'clock; am Montag – **on** Monday; morgens – **in** the morning; nachts – **at** night; im Sommer – **in** summer; an Ostern – **at** Easter; während des Mittagessens – **during** lunch; mittwochs – **on** Wednesdays; am 15. Oktober – **on** 15th October ; nach dem Frühstück – **after** breakfast; an Weihnachten – **at** Christmas

2 a) We have a big brunch **at** the weekend.
b) My friend and I play hockey in the garden **in** the afternoon.
c) I walk to school every day **in** the morning.
d) I love to visit my friends in London **in** December.
e) My parents and I go to Italy **in** winter.

3 *Sue:* "(...) I have looked everywhere **in** my room and it's not **in** the kitchen, either. It's not **on** the shelves and not **in front of** the coffee maker. I even looked **behind** (...)."
Mum: "I think I saw it somewhere **in** the living-room, **next to** the television or **on** the table **between** the TV guide (...)."
Sue: "Ah, there it is! I left it **opposite** the mirror (...)!"

4 um drei Uhr – **at** three o'clock; rund um das Haus – **around** the house; am Dienstag – **on** Tuesday; im März – **in** March; gegen das Fenster – **against** the window; im Frühling – **in** spring; zwischen ein und zwei Uhr – **between** one and two o'clock; am Morgen – **in** the morning; vor dem Abendessen – **before** dinner; am Bahnhof vorbei – **past** the station; während des Frühstücks – **during** breakfast; über die Brücke – **over** the bridge; am Wochenende – **at** the weekend; 2011 – **in** 2011; aus dem Auto steigen – get **out of** the car

5 ordinary → gewöhnlich; ordinär → vulgar
rent → die Miete; Rente → pension
to wonder → sich fragen; sich wundern → to be surprised
personal → persönlich; Personal → staff
receipt → Quittung; Rezept → prescription (Arztrezept)/recipe (Kochrezept)
chips → Pommes Frites; Chips → crisps

6 a) rent; b) criticism; c) opinion; d) meaning – mobile phone/cell phone; e) marks

7 a) prescription; b) staff; c) pension; d) boss

8 a) What's the ~~actual~~ → **current** score? – It's 2:3 for our team.
b) The ~~murder~~ → **murderer** could escape easily.
c) At the moment, (...). It's a very interesting ~~lecture~~ → **reading.**
d) The department store's ~~personal~~ → **staff** is taking a trip to the castle tomorrow.
e) Kate ~~wondered~~ → **was surprised** when Kevin told her about his problems.
Die falsch verwendeten Begriffe und ihre Übersetzung: actual → tatsächlich; murder → Mord; lecture → Vorlesung; personal → persönlich; to wonder → sich fragen

9

BE	**AE**	**deutsche Bedeutung**
crisps	chips	Chips
biscuit	cookie	Keks
film	movie	Film
exercise book	notebook	Übungsheft
lift	elevator	Aufzug
autumn	fall	Herbst
underground	subway	U-Bahn
lorry	truck	Lastwagen
rubbish	trash	Abfall
holiday	vacation	Ferien
petrol	gas	Benzin

10 colour → **color;** theatre → **theater;** monologue → **monolog;** traveling → **travelling;** programme → **program;** flavour → **flavor;** catalogue → **catalog;** to colonialise → **colonialize;** metre → **meter**

11 **Zustimmung äußern:** That's quite right./That's my view exactly./I can't agree with you more./I agree (entirely).
Ablehnung äußern: I don't agree at all./I don't think that's right./I may be wrong but .../That's not the way I see it.
Meinungen erfragen: How do you feel/think about this?/What is your view on the matter?/Do you agree with that?/Would you like to add anything?

12 **Lösungsvorschlag:**
a) I think that teenagers shouldn't have their own TV because young people watch too much TV anyway.
b) I'm sure that something should be done about this problem, but how?
c) I suppose that such a law can't be passed because it is far from realistic.
d) I find it strange that children should be disciplined, but sometimes it is necessary.
e) In my opinion cell phones cannot be banned at schools, because it is impossible to control every single student.

13 You have to look at the pros of cons of legalizing drugs.
At last they agreed with us.
I'm sure that something could be done about animal experiments.

On the one hand, using guns should be legalized, on the other hand, gun control is also necessary.
Cosmetic surgery is no longer for the rich and famous, in other words, everyone can afford it these days.
In conclusion, I would like to thank everyone present.
They looked all very similar, like clones, so to speak.

14 First Jessica appeared at school with pink hair, black clothes and rings on several parts of her body. Next she was sent to the headmaster, who told her that she had failed to bring credit upon herself, the other pupils and the school by her appearance. Finally she wasn't allowed to attend normal lessons, and in conclusion she was excluded from school for a few days. The code of conduct states that pupils must wear a school uniform, in summary, they shouldn't expose themselves.

15 a) building; b) vegetable; c) sports; d) tool; e) toy

16 a) unfortunate; b) terrible; c) truth; d) inactive; e) health; f) youngful; g) impossible; h) unpolite, unmobile

17 to take over → **to control;** appalling → **shocking/bad;** to break out → **to start;** to be involved in → **to take part in;** to be questioned → **to be interrogated;** to be released → **to be set free;** ravenous → **very great;** to dawn on → **to realize;** desperate → **hopeless**

18 a) discuss; b) false, c) horror; d) key; e) lie; f) occur

19 **A:** Aussprache des Wortes; **B:** Wortklasse: Substantiv *(noun);* **C:** Bedeutung des Wortes; **D:** Beispielsatz; **E:** Sprachebene: *informal English*; **F:** grammatikalische Besonderheit: nicht zählbar *(U)*; **G:** Synonym des Wortes; **H:** idiomatische Wendung; **I:** Wortzusammensetzung: Ableitung

10 Umgang mit Texten

2 A short history of movies

3 ***Satzreihenfolge:*** 5 – 2 – 1 – 4 – 6 – 11 – 8 – 14 – 10 – 12 – 3 – 13 – 7 – 9

4 Many teenagers have a dream of becoming a movie star. Freddie Highmore, from London, is only 13 years old, but about to become famous. Already, he has been in eight films of which *Charlie and the Chocolate Factory* has probably been his biggest project so far.
The movie also stars Johnny Depp, one of America's most famous actors. Freddie enjoyed working alongside Johnny Depp and so for Freddie a widespread teenage dream has come true. However, he's still a child and that fact gives him enough coolness to state that he's not sure if he wants to make movies for the rest of his life.

5 a) It's a short text about Freddie Highmore, a British teenager, who is a movie star already.
b) Charlie and the Chocolate Factory
c) acting alongside Johnny Depp
d) At the end, the text tells us that although being quite a star already, Freddie Highmore is not sure whether there are no other challenges for him in life.

6 **Silicon Valley**
Silicon Valley is located on the San Francisco peninsula in California. At the beginning of the 20th century this area was mainly agricultural, dominated by vast orchards. At that time the main industries of the US were on the East Coast and California was regarded as a land of farmers. It was a wonderful sight when in spring the valley was covered with blossoms of many colours. Thus, it was given the name "Valley of Heart's Delight".
Everything changed in the 1930s with Fred Terman. He was a professor at Stanford University's department of electrical engineering, near San Francisco. It troubled him that his graduates could not find employment in California but had to go to the East to get a job. Fred Terman decided to make the "Valley of Delight" into the world's high-tech centre. The US forces were very interested in radio engineering for military reasons and, after World War II, Terman was successful in obtaining money for research from various sources. With this money, Terman was able to attract brilliant students and establish new research departments.
The professor did not only teach his students, but he also encouraged them to start their own companies in the valley. Two of Terman's graduates followed his advice: Bill Hewlett and Dave Packard. In 1939, with ideas in the field of electronics, they founded a firm, the "Hew-

lett-Packard Company". Their first large order was from Walt Disney Productions. It was for making motion pictures more lively.
Today, Hewlett-Packard is one of the world's largest producers of computers and electronic equipment. It currently employs more than 80,000 people worldwide and has sales of more than 6 billion dollars per year.
The great success of Fred Terman also has a tragic aspect: at the age of 24 he fell seriously ill with tuberculosis. Doctors gave him up, but he recovered. He suffered all his life from his illness; at times he was able to work only two hours a day.
Despite his poor health Terman worked with enormous energy. He built up laboratories, new university departments and factories, all at the same place. In the 1950s, he created a huge industrial park with firms such as Eastman Kodak and Fairchild, the latter producing the first semiconductors.
In the 1980s the term "Silicon Valley" was used because the most important products, the semiconductor chips, are made of silicon.
Today the former orchards have given way to the buildings of about 2000 electronics and information technology companies, including the fast-growing field of computers. Silicon Valley is the world centre of high technology.

7 "Silicon Valley" is a non-fictional text about a region along the US-American West Coast. The text gives us information about the industrial development of that region and shows detailed background information on that development.

8 a) Silicon Valley is located on the San Francisco, California, peninsula in the USA.
b) You could find vast orchards there.
c) It was concentrated on the East Coast.
d) It came from the wonderful sight in spring, when the valley was covered with blossoms of many colours.
e) He worked at Stanford University's department of electrical engineering near San Francisco.
f) The US Forces were interested in radio engineering for military reasons.
g) He advised them to start their own companies in the valley.
h) The company produces computers and electronic equipment.
i) You can find laboratories, new university departments, and factories.
j) It comes from the most important products, the semiconductor chips, that are made of silicon.

9 Lösungsvorschlag:
Fred Terman was a professor of electrical engineering, working at Stanford University in California in the 1930s. He appears to have been a very ambitious man with own visions: He believed in the ideas and creativity of his students and not only encouraged them to start their own businesses, but offered real help and assistance by establishing new research departments. And although Fred Terman had fallen quite ill, he succeeded in realizing his plans. His vision became true, and today, Silicon Valley is one of the world centres of high technology.

10 – Before operating the system, **check** that the operating **voltage indicated on the type plate** of your system is **identical with the voltage of your local power supply.** If not, please consult your dealer. The type plate is located at the rear of your system.
– When the system is **switched on,** do **not move it** around.
– **Place** the system in a location with **adequate ventilation** to prevent internal heat build-up in your system. (...)

11 Spannung = **voltage;** beinhalten = **to incorporate;** Wiedergabe = **playback;** Stromversorgung = **power supply;** Standort = **location;** Wandsteckdose = **wall socket**

12 at the rear of → *syn.* **at the back of,** *ant.* **at the front of;** to switch on → *syn.* **to turn on,** *ant.* **to switch/to turn off;** to prevent → *syn.* **to stop,** *ant.* **to cause;** to expose → *syn.* **to show,** *ant.* **to hide;** to invalidate → *syn.* **to weaken,** *ant.* **to validate;** a damp room → *syn.* **a wet room,** *ant.* **a dry room**

13 If your system is not identical with the voltage of your own power supply, **go and see your dealer and ask him/her what to do.**
The system shouldn't be moved around **when it is turned on.**
The system should also not be placed in a location **that is wet, sandy or hot.**
If you don't want the guarantee to become invalid, don't **repair the system yourself.**
If moisture condenses on the lens of the CD, **leave the power on for about an hour with no disc until you can play your CD.**

14 a) You should check whether the voltage of your system is identical with the voltage of your socket.
b) It prevents the system from overheating.
c) Water droplets may be found on the lens of the CD unit inside the system.
d) It won't operate normally if the lens of the CD unit is moist.
e) You can disconnect it by unplugging the AC power plug.

15 a) This text is an advertisement for a new encyclopedia, the "Encyclopedia 2009".
b) The text is about the advantages of the "Encyclopedia 2009". It tells us a lot of facts about the contents and the size of this new encyclopedia. It gives a lot of figures *(Daten, Zahlen)* to impress the readers.
c) The text doesn't name an author, but one can assume that the company which publishes the encyclopedia is responsible for the text.
d) A text like that may be published in various kinds of newspapers, magazines or as a leaflet *(Flugblatt)*.
e) It is written to attract people's attention and to encourage people to buy the encyclopedia.

16 This text which is headlined "Looking for an answer?" is an advertisement for the so-called "Encyclopedia 2009". The readers are given a lot of figures, such as the number of headwords, of visual elements and other contents. The text also mentions the fact that the product *(here: a group term instead of re-using the word "encyclopedia" again)* is based on year-long experience and expertise *(repeat key words!)* and gives two examples of its usefulness: on the one hand, users can get quick access to facts and information, on the other hand detailed information about various subjects is available.
The next paragraph enumerates the encyclopedia's additional advantages: it contains information about recent technologies and innovations as well as an audio-DVD to add even more information.
And as a conclusion, the text encourages the reader to buy the advertised product.

17 **Economic aspects of modern Ireland**
Ireland's economy has long been dominated by agriculture. This is a thing of the past. Industry is the most important sector now, contributing 46 % to the Gross Domestic Product *(Bruttosozialprodukt)*, almost 80 % to exports and employing close to 30 % of the labour force. Industry in Ireland is largely made up of well-known international firms, a lot of them operating in the high-tech sector. Ireland is the world's largest exporter of software and is also home to many producers of computers and computer equipment. A quarter of Europe's computers are made in Ireland by firms like Dell and IBM. One of Intel's largest and most advanced plants is located just outside Dublin.
Economic growth *(wirtschaftliches Wachstum)*, however, also depends on the service industry and tourism. Tourism has a long tradition in Ireland, but today it is call centres, service operations and finance that dominate the economy. Both Apple and IBM located their European customer service operations in Ireland due to *(aufgrund)* the availability of a young, well-educated, English-speaking workforce and a good communications infrastructure. Many people calling a service hotline in Europe or the US are in fact put through to a call centre in Ireland.
Ireland is no longer one of Europe's poorhouses. It has joined Europe's highly developed countries on equal terms.

Lösungsvorschlag:
The text describes the economic situation in modern Ireland. The country used to be dominated by agriculture and is an industrial country today (most important: computer and software industry).
Furthermore, the text informs its readers about tourism and the service industry in Ireland. A lot of international companies maintain big businesses in Ireland due to young and well-trained workers.
The text concludes by saying that Ireland, once a poor country, is now on the same level as its neighbours regarding its economy.

18 I'm a teenager of seventeen. My teenage years haven't really been as good as they could have been; they are over now because I have a baby daughter and I'm a single mother.
By the time my six-month-old daughter will be able to look after herself, I'll be thirty-something, too old to do things that I am now missing out on.
I would love to go clubbing and be like all the other teenagers enjoying themselves: unfortunately, I'll never have these things but I'm the one to be blamed – it's all my fault. I should have taken something to prevent getting pregnant. (...)

topic outline: Meg's reason for being an unhappy teenager, her experince with teenage pregnancy, her relationship with her boyfriend, Meg's future with a baby

19 a) I would be like other teenagers **having fun/having a good time.**
b) I should have **taken the pill/taken something to prevent conception.**
c) His parents **accepted his decision/agreed with him.**
d) My boyfriend **didn't feel responsible/didn't worry about the situation.**
e) I **often went out** almost every night/I **went out on a regular basis.**
f) I think **it's a shame/it's sad that** I haven't done my A-levels yet.

20 a) ... she is a single mother.
b) ... that she can't do the things normal teenagers do at her age.
c) ... doesn't care about the baby.
d) ... the baby will probably limit her future prospects.
e) ... Meg won't be able to go to university.

21 Lösungsvorschlag:
The text is about a seventeen-year-old teenager called Meg who is a single mother. This situation makes her quite unhappy since she can't do the things she used to do, like going out in the evening. She got pregnant from her first boyfriend, who doesn't feel responsible for the baby. Moreover, Meg has realized that she might have spoilt all her prospects for the future because she hasn't done her A-levels. Although she wanted to have the baby, she has some doubts about her future, and she wishes to turn back time.

22 Hi, my name is Laura, and I will be finished with high school in exactly three days. After that I'm free – no looking back. I am seventeen – well, almost eighteen – and have everything to live for. For the eight months before I go to university, I'll have more time on my hands than I'll know what to do with. Maybe I'll tour around Europe. Or perhaps I can travel through America. The possibilities are endless.
I told my parents I wanted to see Vancouver, India and Tibet. I want to see oceans and mountains – jungles and deserts. My mother simply said "fine" as long as I didn't mind being raped and murdered. The world isn't the same as it used to be, she said. (...)

23 Laura is an **adolescent** girl who is most **uncertain** what to do (...). She feels like **trying out** several things, (...). Her mother, however, asks her **to consider** those plans (...). But how can Laura possibly **mature** if she (...)? She doesn't want (...), instead she wants to **make the most** of her life. Laura is eager to escape a life full of **tedious routine.**

24 a) Laura will leave high school very soon, and then she will have plenty of time at her disposal before she goes to university. Although she has a vague idea of what to do, she is not really sure how to spend her time sensibly.
b) Laura's mother reacts in a sort of humorous way. She doesn't mind her daughter travelling the world but Laura should be aware of the dangers she might have to face.
c) Her father is rather practical about that issue. He wants her to consider the financial aspect of travelling around because she might need the money for university. He also seems to be worried as to his daughter's future.
d) She wants to avoid leading a life that is meaningless. She feels like experiencing something exciting and new. She would hate ending up like most people: school – university – job and so on.
e) She suggests that you should make plans for the future, but you shouldn't listen to other people's advice and suggestions. You should only do what is best for you, thus what might make you happy in the end because then you won't regret anything.

25 Laura, a teenager who will have finished her final exams soon, is talking about her lifer after school. She is considering travelling the world, but her parents are trying to dissuade her. Whereas her mother is talking about possible risks, her father has a rather practical approach to the problem: money might be a problem, since he wants her to go to university. Laura, however, is of the opinion that you should do the things you want to do no matter what other people might say.

27 a) the characters; b) first-person narrator; c) point of view; d) limited in her knowledge; e) feelings, thoughts and motives; f) mood and talent permit; g) can't be fully trusted; h) emotional account of the events

28 a) → *true*
b) → *false; correct answer:* As a protagonist, Gemma is also a round character.

LÖSUNGEN

c) → *false; correct answer:* Gemma is characterized implicitly through what she does, thinks and says.
d) → *false; correct answer:* It becomes quite obvious that the relationship with her parents is far from being close because she isn't of the same opinion as her parents. There is a conflict between Gemma and her parents.

29 a) The text at hand presents a conflict between a teenager and her parents.
b) Gemma doesn't speak highly of her parents. She thinks that they haven't done a great job in bringing her up. They are clueless and incompetent; they simply failed in being proper parents.
c) Gemma's point of view is presented. She is the narrator – the first-person narrator. As a consequence, only her thoughts and feelings are shown, and we don't know whether she can be fully trusted. Her perspective is also quite limited and subjective.
d) Gemma is presented indirectly/implicitly. We get to know her through what she says and how she treats her parents. The basic traits of her character are being rebellious, quarrelsome and impatient, because she is strongly opposed to what her parents say and think. The way she argues with them is quite aggressive and impatient. But the conversation with her parents also shows that she is determined and straightforward. She calls a spade a spade, and she always insists on her opinion.

31 *Flashback:* The first-person narrator is a schoolboy when a new boy from Germany attends school. Gradually the German boy is learning English, but apparently he is homesick. He cries every night, and all of a sudden he refuses to speak English. In the end, he is sent home.
The present: When the first-person narrator is in his office, he is seeing a woman standing in the rain. While watching, he remembers Klaus, the German boy who was once in his class. This situation makes him think about Klaus.

32 **"I":** the narrator – first person narrator which means that he is a character in the story – one of the main characters; he is portrayed as being friendly, good-natured and sensitive
Klaus: the protagonist who initiates the conflict because he is foreign; he is described as being sensitive, sad, desperate and fearful
the woman: a minor character that triggers off the flashbacks; she might be depressed or sad; "miserable" is mentioned at one point
the headmaster: a minor character; he introduces Klaus to the class; we get some details about his face and thus his health; he dies of a sunstroke

34 a) short play; b) playwrights; c) stage directions; d) stage properties; e) characters; f) dialogue; g) performed on stage

35

characters	outward appearance	words/ thoughts/ behaviour
headmaster	a tweed suit/formal/gentlemen-like	talks to Mr Perkins in a superior way/uses a lot of words having to do with violence and death/doesn't take Mr Perkins seriously
Mr Perkins	neatly dressed/a sports-jacket	inferior to the headmaster/short sentences, a lot of questions showing that he is not in charge/feeling helpless

characters	feelings/ attitudes	other important details
headmaster	furious and angry/is all for a strict punishment/a disciplinarian with queer attitudes	is in charge because he is the headmaster
Mr Perkins	shocked and frightened/upset and worried/concerned/nervous/accepts authorities	is degraded by the headmaster

36 The Headmaster, one of the protagonists, is in charge of the whole situation. This is not only shown by his outward appearance. He is formally dressed in a tweed suit. He looks like a gentleman, which stands in a clear contrast to his behaviour towards Mr Perkins. The way he talks to Mr Perkins underlines his characteristic features. He seems to have some queer attitudes when it comes to discipline and punishment – he is all for a severe punishment; but when there is a casualty (Tommy) he plays the situation down and becomes rather sarcastic. Mr Perkins, also a protagonist, is obviously inferior to the headmaster. Though he is neatly dressed, he is only dressed in a sports jacket. He is the one who puts forward plenty of questions, thus he feels rather helpless and exposed to this weird headmaster. He seems to accept the headmaster and his authority. He is just shocked and upset on hearing about Tommy's fate.

37 In the short play Fatal Beatings by Ben Elton and Richard Curtis, the headmaster of a school has asked Mr Perkins to come to his office. Mr Perkins' son Tommy is in trouble because he has been disobedient recently. Among other things Tommy hasn't done his work properly and he has also taken some books from the library without a library card. So the headmaster had to punish him severely. It was too severe as it turns out because Tommy dropped dead while bending over to be hit. The headmaster tries to play down the whole situation by making sarcastic comments on Tommy's death.

39 a) The poem is divided into four stanzas/verses. The first three stanzas consist of four lines, whereas the last stanza consists of one line only.
b) There are rhymes in each stanza – except the last one: there are end rhymes – the second and the fourth line of each stanza rhyme.
c) The poet repeats some words such as "and" or "they get" at the beginning of almost every line. He also uses alliterations such as "gunfire, ... growling, and glee" or metaphors such as "blood ... flowing over the screen".

40 *zutreffend:* a), b), d), f)

41 I love it when ≈ It's a pleasure when
they can't hold a scream ≈ they cry out
the audience trembles ≈ the people watching shake
I don't like people kissing ≈ I detest people kissing

42 The speaker likes it when there is gunfire, when people are dead, when heroes are winning and the bad guys die slowly and when there ist a lot of blood to be seen = twelve lines
He doesn't like it when people kiss = one line

43 The poem contains two contrasting statements. One statements is introduced by "I love it when ...", whereas the second one begins with "But I don't like ...". The speaker presents a long list of things he enjoys seeing. Apparently he can't get enough violence. He gives a lot of examples of atrocities and reveals minute details. However, he states his dislikes in only one summary sentence. This final statement comes as a complete surprise and is rather shocking. It suggests that the speaker is unable to show feelings of affection and tenderness. He cannot even talk about such feelings (one line only), but he finds a lot of expressions and words for violent scenes (twelve lines).

Register

Das 3-fach-Prinzip für bessere Noten

Die Lernhilfenreihe „Einfach klasse in“ für die 5. bis 10. Klasse überzeugt durch ihren besonderen Aufbau:

- Übersichtlich strukturiert in die drei Lernbausteine **Wissen – Üben – Testen**
- Alle wichtigen Lernbereiche einer Klassenstufe in einem Band zusammengefasst
- Mit persönlichem Klassenarbeitsplaner
- Nach den neuesten Bildungsplänen der Bundesländer entwickelt

DEUTSCH

Einfach klasse in
Deutsch 5. Klasse
ISBN 978-3-411-72151-1

Einfach klasse in
Deutsch 6. Klasse
ISBN 978-3-411-72161-0

Einfach klasse in
Deutsch 7. Klasse
ISBN 978-3-411-72251-8

Einfach klasse in
Deutsch 8. Klasse
ISBN 978-3-411-72261-7

Einfach klasse in
Deutsch 9. Klasse
ISBN 978-3-411-72411-6

Einfach klasse in
Deutsch 10. Klasse
ISBN 978-3-411-72421-5

ENGLISCH

Einfach klasse in
Englisch 5. Klasse
ISBN 978-3-411-72131-3

Einfach klasse in
Englisch 6. Klasse
ISBN 978-3-411-72141-2

Einfach klasse in
Englisch 7. Klasse
ISBN 978-3-411-72271-6

Einfach klasse in
Englisch 8. Klasse
ISBN 978-3-411-72281-5

Einfach klasse in
Englisch 9. Klasse
ISBN 978-3-411-72591-5

Einfach klasse in
Englisch 10. Klasse
ISBN 978-3-411-72601-1

MATHEMATIK

Einfach klasse in
Mathematik 5. Klasse
ISBN 978-3-411-72171-9

Einfach klasse in
Mathematik 6. Klasse
ISBN 978-3-411-72181-8

Einfach klasse in
Mathematik 7. Klasse
ISBN 978-3-411-72431-4

Einfach klasse in
Mathematik 8. Klasse
ISBN 978-3-411-72441-3

Einfach klasse in
Mathematik 9. Klasse
ISBN 978-3-411-72571-7

Einfach klasse in
Mathematik 10. Klasse
ISBN 978-3-411-72581-6

FRANZÖSISCH

Einfach klasse in
Französisch 1. Lernjahr
ISBN 978-3-411-72741-4

Einfach klasse in
Französisch 2. Lernjahr
ISBN 978-3-411-72751-3

Einfach klasse in
Französisch 3./4. Lernjahr
ISBN 978-3-411-72821-3

LATEIN

Einfach klasse in
Latein 1. Lernjahr
ISBN 978-3-411-72721-6

Einfach klasse in
Latein 2. Lernjahr
ISBN 978-3-411-72731-5

Einfach klasse in
Latein 3./4. Lernjahr
ISBN 978-3-411-72811-4

Jeder Band:
128 Seiten. Kartoniert, mit Umschlagklappen